BUSINESS PRESENTATIONS
THAT PERSUADE, ENGAGE & GET RESULTS

OWN THE ROOM

David Booth • Deborah Shames • Peter Desberg

Mc
Graw
Hill

New York   Chicago   San Francisco   Lisbon   London   Madrid   Mexico City
Milan   New Delhi   San Juan   Seoul   Singapore   Sydney   Toronto

The McGraw-Hill Companies

Library of Congress Cataloging-in-Publication Data

Booth, David.
　　Own the room : business presentations that persuade, engage, and get results /
David Booth, Peter Desberg, and Deborah Shames.
　　　　p.　　cm.
　　ISBN 978-0-07-162859-4 (alk. paper)
　　1. Business presentations.　　I. Desberg, Peter.　　II. Shames, Deborah.
　　III. Title.

HF5718.22.B66　　2010
658.4′52—dc22　　　　　　　　　　　　　　　　　　　　　　　　2009014682

1　2　3　4　5　6　7　8　9　10　11　12　13　14　15　16　17　18　19　20　FGR/FGR　0　9

ISBN　　978-0-07-162859-4
MHID　　　0-07-162859-2

McGraw-Hill books are available at special quantity discounts to use as premiums and
sales promotions or for use in corporate training programs. To contact a representative,
please e-mail us at bulksales@mcgraw-hill.com.

This book is printed on acid-free paper.

Contents

Preface

We think that 7 A.M. business meetings, fueled by mediocre coffee and cold bagels, are a cruel and unusual form of punishment. The most painful part isn't the food—it's when members of our networking organization stand up to introduce themselves. "I'm Michael Doyle with Berber, Flushing and Doyle, LLC. We're a full-service accounting firm, catering to high-net-worth individuals and midsized businesses. We really care about our clients and help them solve the issues that keep them up at night." Then they repeat their name, title, and company as if they are reciting their name, rank, and serial number.

After twenty-five or so similar introductions, suicide begins to look like an attractive option. In self-defense, we decided to fight back. We had been working as communication consultants in Silicon Valley, training engineers in the technology industry to clearly explain product functions to their sales and marketing teams. We thought that techno-speak was the height of insider jargon disguised as English. We were wrong. Engineers are not the only professionals who rely on clinical, analytical data to express what they do in a way that only other engineers understand. The same holds true for service providers, retail specialists, and executives in other fields.

After relocating Eloqui, the communication company we founded in 1999, to Los Angeles, we began to train accountants, lawyers, and financial advisors to improve their communication skills, starting with the way they introduced themselves. Instead of the boring, drab introductions they had been reciting for years, we encouraged them to differentiate their services and to include client anecdotes with vivid details and personal insights. These novel elevator speeches became viral. If someone reverted to the default mode of introduction, he would be upstaged by the next professional who creatively described her product or services. Time and again these professionals came back to us, looking for new and innovative ways to introduce themselves, deal with clients more effectively, and better their communication to achieve their objectives. Finally, we began to look forward to these self-introductions. It was fun to watch professionals compete with each other. And as their introductions became memorable, more business resulted—they began to see results almost immediately. The group could now picture what everyone did for a living, what set them apart, and who would be an appropriate client referral.

Unfortunately, a brief elevator speech is a lot easier to repair than an hour-long presentation. Yesterday, for example, we sat in a room for more than an hour listening to a PowerPoint presentation on computer forensics directed toward law firms. The speaker, Steven, was from a large accounting firm with a high-profile name which he leveraged to draw in a captive audience. He began by thanking those in attendance and then outlining his agenda, meticulously detailing what he was going to talk about. He then presented a fifteen-minute "commercial" about his company's abilities, resources, and client list. He cared. We didn't. Up to this point, the focus of Steven's presentation was on himself and his company, not what everyone else was concerned about—themselves.

For his sixty-minute presentation, Steven constructed fifty-eight PowerPoint slides. The title of each slide was hardly riveting. Try sitting through "Analytic and Forensic Technology Overview" followed by "Overall Strategy for Data Analysis." Although Steven had well-supported evidence for every point, he was led by the content. He never grabbed anyone's attention with visual details, an arresting opening, or his personal observations. He failed to infuse the presentation with actual anecdotes or demonstrate his role in the process. Although he presented a thorough analysis of how data could be corrupted, stolen, or improperly used, he failed to address the specific challenges that lawyers were facing—which was why they had come to hear him. The first example of direct application to a legal case didn't appear until slide forty-eight. Steven was at least forty slides too late.

His vocal delivery didn't help the situation either. He never changed the speed, volume, or pitch of his voice. He assumed the audience was expecting a "professional" delivery, which to him meant void of color, enthusiasm, and as little emphasis as possible. Although it lasted only sixty minutes, it was the longest afternoon of our lives. And as we looked around the room, none of the lawyers was paying much attention either. Some were reading, while others were glued to their Blackberrys—with the accompanying sound of thumbs clicking away on tiny keyboards. Steven paid double for failing to engage his audience. He not only picked up the tab for the room *and* the lawyers' lunch, but he also lost a valuable opportunity to generate new business.

Steven had played it safe. Years ago, the *Los Angeles Times Magazine* had an interview with a salesman from Brooks Brothers who said something very revealing. He pointed out that people did not shop at Brooks Brothers because they liked the clothes. They shopped there because they didn't want to dress incorrectly. They knew that if they wore a Brooks Brothers suit to a board meeting, they wouldn't make a mistake. Steven did his best not to make a mistake with his presentation.

Books on communication tend to take the Brooks Brothers approach. If you do what they say, they claim you won't make a mistake. You won't stand out or be criticized. This is a shortsighted recipe for conquering fear. But this approach doesn't work because it is not the most effective way to communicate. We do not believe there is a one-size-fits-all method to successful presentations. Good communication is personal, revealing, and memorable. It persuades, influences, and makes you indelible in the minds of your audience. We want people to look forward to speaking, mesmerizing audiences, and attaining their goals.

The traditional approach to public speaking is also based on rules. Countless books have lists of dos and don'ts, such as the following:

- Gesture with one hand and keep the other in your pocket.
- Stand behind the podium to convey authority.
- A pause means you don't know your subject, so never pause.
- Don't touch anything above your neck.

If Will Rogers had followed the presentation standard of his time, he would not have been the most popular speaker of his generation or have been asked to entertain U.S. presidents. Winston Churchill also broke stylistic rules and inspired an entire nation through World War II. During the 2008 presidential campaign, Barack Obama captivated audiences by speaking from the heart, revealing the difficulties of growing up in a racially mixed family, and employing eloquent rhetoric that touched a wide spectrum of the voting public.

Rules are useful for writing a computer program, but they don't provide guidance in communication. When you examine history, the greatest scientists, artists, and inventors all had one thing in common—they broke the rules. We prefer guidelines to rules, because every presentation contains unique elements. The Eloqui method of persuasive speaking embodies these concepts:

- Strive to speak in an authentic voice from your own perspective.
- Identify one primary intention and shape your content around it.
- Persuade your audience by using a variety of engagement techniques rather than by simply educating or informing.

- Grab and keep your audience's attention, beginning with your opening remarks.
- Use imagery and visual snapshots to support facts and figures.
- Whenever possible, use examples to illustrate, clarify, and support your ideas.
- Close with commitment, certainty, and a robust final statement.

HOW THIS BOOK CAME TO BE WRITTEN

Most books on presentation skills emanate from PR or advertising executives, "educators" in the field of "communication," or are written by successful public speakers who share their personal tips and techniques. At the time of this writing, there were approximately fifteen hundred books dealing with public speaking listed on Amazon.com. Most of these books present traditional rules for speaking etiquette and communication. Enter stage left: David Booth and Deborah Shames—performer and director with their own methodology.

David Booth

David was a professional theater director and classically trained actor. Over the course of his career, he performed countless plays in theater repertoires—from Shakespeare to Ibsen. He was one of the original members of the Berkeley Rep as well as the Tennessee Williams Center. David taught theater arts at the university and college level, including Virginia Commonwealth University and the Pacific Conservatory of the Performing Arts. Although a great deal of his background was in performing, this story really began when he started working as a spokesman for large corporations such as Siemens Medical, Bank of America, Chevron, and Cisco Systems.

It was as a corporate spokesman that David witnessed firsthand the cookie-cutter approach executives used to make presentations.

They were all dependent on virtually the same tools. These included a conservative business suit and a tightly prepared script—which was often an exact replica of the PowerPoint presentation projected behind the speaker.

Almost everyone in the companies he worked for presented in a safe, conventional way. The formula for delivering presentations focused on the superficial, such as gestures, body language, and eye contact. David rebelled against the conservative uniform, tedious script, and dry delivery. He began to conceptualize and practice a methodology that would make him stand out. David combined his acting experience with corporate presentation skills to produce a more authentic and compelling style.

The old paradigm bred self-consciousness and a fear of making mistakes. The new paradigm that David developed married emotional with cognitive persuasion. Many companies now realize that in today's competitive marketplace, the goal is to be unique and memorable rather than take a defensive posture of not being wrong.

Deborah Shames

In the mid-1990s, David joined forces with Deborah Shames—an award-winning producer and director. Deborah had years of experience behind the camera, directing and producing several independent films and more than sixty corporate training and educational videos.

She had directed luminaries including Wendie Malick, Rita Moreno, Danny Glover, and Angela Lansbury. To launch three of her independent films, she formed the video distribution company Deborah Films. Working with female executives and authors, she observed a heightened level of anxiety whenever women presented before large audiences or on camera, and she developed techniques to shift the emphasis from listening to the inner critic to engaging the audience.

Deborah and David understand the role of actors is to intellectually engage and emotionally affect their audiences and recognized that this is also the goal of every presenter. Together, they developed a series of training techniques based on directing, acting, and theater arts principles. Combining their extensive experience in the entertainment industry and corporate arena, they formed Eloqui, coaching individuals and training teams within corporations to differentiate their services and apply effective communication skills. Now there are a number of Eloqui trainers, each working to enhance clients' unique speaking style, who integrate performance techniques with applied cognitive science research, and deliver practical tools that give professionals the means to effectively persuade any audience.

Eloqui has trained executives at TD Ameritrade, Amgen, Mattel, Fisher-Price, Merrill Lynch, Pfizer, Intuit, Greenberg Glusker, Paul Hastings, and Sun Microsystems, to name a few. Then David and Deborah met Peter Desberg.

Peter Desberg

Peter is a licensed clinical psychologist and university professor who specializes in stage fright. He has authored twenty books and numerous book chapters and is a popular presenter at professional conferences. He has done extensive research in the areas of public speaking, performance anxiety, and instructional humor. Peter has worked with well-known actors, athletes, and musicians, as well as business professionals to overcome anxiety and enhance their performance. Since the mid-1990s, he has also hosted a cable TV program on technology.

When Peter joined David and Deborah, they seamlessly merged his psychological principles and academic research with their field experience and entertainment knowledge.

By combining performance techniques and cognitive science with the best research in psychology, *Own the Room* will guide you in delivering any presentation, provide tools to manage anxiety, and ensure that audiences will remember you and your message.

Acknowledgments

DAVID AND DEBORAH OF ELOQUI

To our accountant, Gary Notti, who long ago told us we should team up and form a communication training company. We foolishly ignored his advice for years, until we caved in, teamed up profession-ally *and* personally, and toasted Gary at our wedding.

Thanks to our dear friend Jeff Prather, who we enlisted to name our company after marketing professionals failed. In his ultimate wisdom, over a bottle of wine, he asked, "What's the origin of elo-quence? That's what you should call your company." Eloqui was born.

We thank Jack Grapes, an extraordinary poet and writing teacher, for making the concept of "write like you talk" come alive. He trans-formed our writing and ensured Eloqui would train clients to speak the same way—with candor, vivid details, and authenticity.

There have been many guides along the way.

David's acting teacher, Irene Comer, danced in fifty cities in fifty days as a young hoofer, and at seventy she could still mop the floor with college students. She taught David the value of physical technique and to study classical Greek theater for the origins of formal speaking and movement.

Laven Sowell, opera singer and mentor, retuned David's hearing and reshaped his voice. He is forever grateful to Laven for the loss of his Oklahoma accent and giving him the solo in his concert choir.

Majoring in Anthropology at the University of Wisconsin and studying filmmaking at the Anthropology Film Center in Santa Fe resulted in Deborah's ability to see the world through stories, culture, and the true voice of each character.

Deborah's craft group of girls (now radiant young women) taught her to facilitate, to be supportive, and most of all, by applying the art of distraction, to create mini-masterpieces.

More recently, Dr. Mark Goulston, author and former FBI hostage negotiator, forced us to be better trainers by fiercely testing our conclusions and theories. He also graciously introduced us to an agent, Bill Gladstone of Waterside Productions, who connected us with McGraw-Hill, which made this book possible.

We greatly appreciate our editors at McGraw-Hill, John Aherne and Nancy Hall. John's supportive and witty comments clarified our thinking and eased the pain of necessary edits. Nancy kindly pointed out our inconsistencies, grammatical errors, and our tendency to repeat ourselves. If she was not entirely successful, the fault lies in us.

Business mentors instrumental in Eloqui's success are Sheri Adams, Mark Lefko, Brian and Jerri Hemsworth, Larry Braun, and Lee Greenberg. They have motivated us to construct effective business models, negotiate with grace, and stay flexible in any economy.

Thank you, Los Angeles ProVisor members for welcoming two Northern Californians and becoming our professional and personal extended community. By attending our workshops, you drove us to turn intellectual concepts into practical skills for clients across diverse industries.

Special thanks to Dr. Lilli Friedland, psychologist and president of Executive Advisors, for introducing us to Dr. Peter Desberg, without whom the science in this book would be only an assumption.

Eloqui trainers Jeannie Alan, Mark Jaffe, and William Hall, seasoned professionals in their own right, absorbed the Eloqui method, made it their own, and advanced the breadth of our firm with elegance and joy.

To our moms: thank you Mickey, for convincing me that being awarded "most talkative" in grade school was really an asset. And Helen for pushing me to become a lawyer, which I never became but frequently played on television.

And to all of you—hundreds of clients, friends, family, and persistent readers of our Eloqui "Tip of the Week"—we are eternally grateful.

DR. PETER DESBERG

I want to thank Dr. Lilli Friedland for being my friend and colleague, in that order. Her introduction to Deborah and David expanded my horizons on presenting and showed me that in the phrase "comfort zone" the word *comfort* is a synonym for *boring*.

I would like to thank our agent, Bill Gladstone, for putting us together with McGraw-Hill, and our editor, John Aherne, for his tireless work in making our efforts translate into readable copy.

I also want to thank my friend and coauthor of our forthcoming humor book, Jeffrey Davis, for modeling good writing and putting up with my clumsy imitation of it as he continues to inspire, instruct, and—did I already say, inspire?

Finally, I want to thank my wife, Cheryll, and daughter, Lauren, who keep a picture of me handy so they can remember what I look like and occasionally come upstairs to visit me as I try to nail down an elusive phrase or example in the search for clarity.

Intention

The Driving Force

I've never understood the rationale for putting your hand through a block of wood. As a woman, it sounds unnecessary and painful. However, Peter explained that breaking wood is an essential part of martial arts training. He makes the case that the exercise teaches two important concepts that also apply to presentation skills: focus and intention. To put your hand through a horizontal piece of wood, you have to visualize as your target, *not* the top surface, but rather a point below it. That means you have to focus on striking two feet below the board with the intention of going right through. You can't hold back. You have to know exactly where you are going and believe that you will get there.

Peter also explained that you do not strike the board with the entire ridge of your hand. You use the heavy bone at the inside and bottom, just above your wrist. Why? Because you focus on one small area to get the most force from the energy you expend. If you succeed, you feel no pain and the wood breaks neatly in half. The corollary is also useful. If you don't follow these rules, you don't break the board, and your hand really hurts.

Delivering a strong presentation is similar to breaking a board. To succeed, you must make an impact. To make an impact, you must have a clear intention. (Note: We use the terms *intention* and *objective* interchangeably.)

You have to know exactly where and how you are going to hit the board. In the same way, your entire presentation should focus on one well-defined intention. Commit all of your resources to this one target. The more intentions you bring into your presentation, the more you dilute the focus and diminish your effectiveness. The audience can't get a handle on where you are going or what you want, making it less likely that you will achieve your objective.

> Speakers must have a clear intention.

Once you clarify your intention, it provides a target for your talk. If you don't, you end up meandering. The martial arts analogy provides another parallel. If your intention is to "fight well," does that mean trying to seriously injure or humiliate your opponent, or teaching your opponent a lesson? From a positive perspective, it could mean trying to be graceful or maintaining a spiritual attitude. So, "fighting well" conveys a lack of clarity. It is a general not a specific objective. You would prepare, practice, and deliver your skills very differently for whichever intention you choose. Your choice would be based on your personal ability, as well as your opponent. It is the same when you deliver a presentation.

When I ask speakers what their intention is or what they would like to achieve, they often respond, "I want to educate or inform my audience." But educating is not persuading. Educating causes people to think; persuading motivates them to act. When speakers' primary intention is to inform or educate their audience, they typically ramble and cover too much information. They present an

> Choose a specific not a general intention.

encyclopedic version of a topic or throw the kitchen sink at the listener to make sure nothing is left out. Their presentation often ends up unfocused and driven by data, instead of a clear narrative with specific examples. And listeners end up being passive, because no interactivity is asked of them.

After our clients realize that educating or informing is a weak intention, they will typically say their objective is to land the business. If that is the case, what is the specific *action* you would like your listeners to take? Is it to refer you to their other clients? To see you as a trusted advisor who provides resources in other areas of their business? Or to let you assemble a team that can take care of their needs?

Suppose, for example, that you are pitching a potential client about the benefits of low-cost/high-coverage group medical insurance. If your intention is centered on having the client see you as the go-to person for providing medical insurance, it should be reflected in every aspect of your presentation. You tell anecdotes about other clients for whom you reduced expenses, increased worker loyalty, and maximized productivity by providing a customized insurance plan. If these anecdotes are similar to the potential client's challenges, she will connect the dots. She will put herself in the picture and extrapolate how you can best serve her needs.

But if your intention is to *inform* them about group medical insurance, you would typically provide statistics on the rising cost of health care, describe the different types of plans in great detail, and outline their costs. You would leave out the anecdotes of how you solved the problem for other clients, because you might believe these examples are irrelevant, when in fact, they are the most persuasive factor in the client's decision-making process.

Persuade your listeners; don't educate them.

Note that if you only inform, you will have achieved that intention, but potential clients will not be motivated to work with you. You have failed to give them the opportunity to see your value or involvement in the process. They may respect your expertise, but you have not *persuaded* them to initiate a relationship. In my experience working with clients in all industries, intention is critical. It is the driving force of every presentation.

It doesn't seem possible that you would make a presentation without knowing what you wanted to achieve, any more than you wouldn't know what you were going to say. There's a wonderful old axiom: "If you don't know where you're going, you may wind up somewhere else." I am stunned at the number of presentations in which the speaker drifts along and the audience has to guess what the message is. Well-organized content is not the same as intention or objective. To be effective, a speaker must keep the intended message in focus throughout the presentation.

Adam Kimmel, the cinematographer for the film *Capote*, put it this way: "I think it's really important to have a mantra or road map visually for a film. I'm always trying to define that, so when you get into a situation where you're walking in cold or under a time constraint or something changes, that you remember what it is that led you to your original idea."

I've heard clients say that ten minutes into a talk, they were just getting around to what was important (that is, their intention) and were told their time was up. I've heard people speed up to include more content or change direction but fail to persuade their audience to take action. I've also heard speakers end with, "Well, I guess that's all. Uh, questions?" In each case, the problem was not their content but the lack of a clear intention.

BULL'S-EYE

Peter was teaching a Fear of Public Speaking class and asked each participant to identify the intention of their presentation. A capable young woman, Marcia, gave seminars on how to put on weddings. Peter asked who attended these seminars, and Marcia said they were engaged couples who believed they couldn't afford professional services like hers. Her intention was to inform the attendees about wedding planning.

Peter pointed out that wedding planning must be very simple if she could teach a bunch of novices all she knew in one day. Marcia fiercely disagreed, saying there was always too much to cover. With a little more prodding, she finally realized that her *true* intention was to overwhelm the attendees so they would feel the need to hire a professional to plan their upcoming weddings. Marcia intuitively knew she was already doing this, but once she became clear on her intention, she was able to scare the daylights out of them by lunch. Then her afternoon was spent describing the different ways she packaged her skills to serve them for a reasonable fee.

Once you identify your intention, like Marcia did, you can't help but rethink your presentation. Marcia radically revised her opening. Instead of giving an overview of wedding planning activities, she immediately involved the attendees by asking them to call out examples of disasters they'd witnessed when they'd attended other weddings.

People started talking about wilted flowers, music that was too loud, and inappropriate, ugly dresses. The list went on for ten minutes. Although the attendees were laughing at the examples, they were also scaring themselves into realizing how many things really could go wrong. With humor and group participation, Marcia had already achieved a big part of her intention. Furthermore, it made everything she said more credible, because the audience had provided the examples.

One Primary Intention

When you begin to construct your talk and consider what to include and what to leave out, you will probably think of many intentions. Narrow your focus. As you examine each possibility, identify the central idea; everything else is a means to achieving that end. Once you have chosen your objective, look at the content that supports it and edit out everything that is not essential. Your intention should be so clear that it can be stated in a single, active sentence. In Hollywood, a writer strives to pitch a movie idea in one short phrase like "A big luxury liner hits a glacier and sinks."

To jump-start your thinking, begin with a phrase such as one of the following:

- "I want . . ."
- "I am going to . . ."
- "We will . . ."
- "They will see me as the . . ."

Remember, the most effective intentions are *active*, not passive.

Ironically, the most effective intentions are also unspoken. Resist the temptation to say it aloud or put it on your agenda slide. This will force you to focus and find more creative ways to present your content. Repeat your intention to yourself right before you speak. Typically, our anxiety peaks in the moments before speaking. By repeating your single intention, instead of trying to recall the entire content of your talk, you will feel more grounded and directed.

> Establish one clear, active intention.

An End Goal

Use an if-then construction to determine if you have achieved your objective. For example, before delivering a presentation to a professional group, your intention would focus on generating new business. So to gauge your success, you would say to yourself, "*If* I am successful, *then* at least three people in the audience will ask for my business card." Or half a dozen people will sign up for the event or workshop you're conducting. Or an executive will approach you to set up his limited liability corporation. Be specific about your anticipated outcome and devise a methodology to evaluate your success.

Unspoken Intentions

If you are having difficulty choosing an active intention, try this exercise. Start with your first thought, like "I will educate this client's representatives about my services." Then ask yourself, "If they are educated, what will happen?" The answer to that question brings you closer to your intention. For example, "Once they are educated, they will identify which of our services they need." Now go down another level and ask yourself, "Once they identify the appropriate services, then what happens?" If the answer is, "They will set up a meeting to discuss how well we know their industry and how we can best serve their needs," getting this meeting may be your true intention.

You may need to go down yet another level to assess whether the fit is right. For example, you may determine that a potential client is too difficult and requires too much time and effort. Or you may determine that the projected time frame is so far in the future (or doesn't exist because the company is fishing) that working together is unlikely. Or the firm may actually be looking for services that are outside your area of expertise.

In business, you may revise your intention at each step in the process, but you should have only one intention per presentation, interaction, or meeting. Once you have identified your intention, you can determine how successful you are in achieving it.

After you have identified the action you want your audience to take, develop a metric to determine if your goals have been met and your intention realized. You can calculate how many people asked to meet for lunch, how many books you sold, or even how many people came up afterward and complimented your talk. The key is to make your metric *observable* and *measurable*. Then you can use this information to evaluate

Gauge your success.

your performance and make future presentations more effective and targeted.

Intention and Persuasion

Traditional public speaking courses identify three types of talks: informative, entertaining, and persuasive. I believe there is only one type—persuasive. If you are giving an informative talk, your intention is still to persuade the audience you know enough to be hired for your expertise. If you are entertaining, then you are persuading listeners that you can be called on for events that need a keynote speaker or master of ceremonies.

Within our networking organization, David and I travel to many chapters and deliver a brief fifteen-minute presentation on how to craft compelling elevator speeches, which are self-introductions or verbal calling cards, short descriptions of you, your services, and your company. Our presentation is interactive and informative, and we don't include a commercial about Eloqui services. But our intention is strong; it is not to educate. We want to persuade at least two members to hire Eloqui for individual and corporate training or to refer us to their clients.

To that end, we give away techniques and intellectual property about messaging, opening, using visual details, and personalizing services. We ask for volunteers and then work with that individual's specific elevator speech. For example, one woman stood up and delivered her traditional elevator speech: "I'm Judith Taylor of Taylor and Associates. I help people find money that's owed them by conducting a licensing audit or using other investigative tools. I work with CPAs, licensing agents, and attorneys to make sure companies recover money due them, like royalties."

Judith was accurate in her description of what she did to serve her clients. Unfortunately, since audience members could not picture how she operated, they had no idea when to bring her in, who her ideal clients were, or how she went about collecting monies owed. Even though people listened intently, they quickly forgot what

Judith did for a living and, more importantly, what referrals they might have.

Personally, Judith had a very colorful style that she entirely sublimated—believing it was unprofessional in a business setting. She loved telling stories but believed that storytelling was considered "soft" and listeners wouldn't think she was credible. We encouraged Judith to move outside her comfort zone, tell a story that would immediately draw us in, and then link that anecdote to what she did for her clients. Reviving her Brooklyn accent, here's Judith's new speech:

> The weeds had taken over my front lawn. Rather than call in a work crew, I decided to clear the brush myself—in accordance with county guidelines. Unfortunately, I set out wearing diamond earrings and bare hands. The job was messy, noisy, and difficult. I loved it. Afterward, I sat back and surveyed the lawn.
>
> That's when I realized I was missing a diamond earring and had dirt under my fingernails. Men have known this for years, but there is a right accessory for every job. In this case, gardening gloves! I also realized that I am an accessory to accountants and attorneys with clients who have royalties owed them and need to be investigated. I find missing monies and put them back in my clients' pockets. And even though it was like looking for a needle in a haystack, I dove into the garbage pail, went through all the weeds, and found my missing earring. I'm Judith Taylor of Taylor and Associates.

Once the assembled professionals responded positively to her new elevator speech, Judith never returned to a generic description. She didn't need to say she was tenacious in collecting the monies owed her clients. They drew their own conclusions by how she attacked the weeds and found her missing earring.

But this exercise was also valuable for *our* credibility. By demonstrating how Judith set herself apart, we gave the assembled professionals a practical demonstration of how Eloqui works. Although the focus of our presentation was delivering techniques for better elevator speeches, we were achieving our intention of persuading individuals to hire us to set themselves apart. By seeing what we did for Judith, listeners could identify and picture themselves in an Eloqui session—and imagine crafting their own compelling elevator speech.

Shape the Content

We were called in to work with Doug, a senior executive at the leading mortgage lending company in the United States. Doug had a major speech coming up to be delivered to his top sales producers. The mortgage industry was facing a rocky time—with expectations of stalled housing starts, rising interest rates, increased competition, and home prices that were considered unsustainably high. It was Doug's intention to motivate the sales force to maintain their leadership position. As part of the speech, he would also applaud their efforts over the past year.

In the past, Doug had given similar speeches based on a traditional business model. He would run the numbers, provide rallying points, and quote business gurus such as Peter Drucker on sound business principles and practices. He would then detail the group's achievements using PowerPoint graphs and charts. The form and structure were recognizable and predictable and therefore lacked the impact (and motivation) Doug was hoping to deliver. His focus had been on educating the sales force rather than persuading them to action.

David and I interviewed Doug about his personal motivation to succeed and maintain his company's leadership position. Surprisingly, we found that he was reticent regarding his upbringing or his career as an NFL wide receiver. Although Doug would occasionally include his philosophy and commitment to the company in his speeches, he never said why and how he had arrived at his present position and level of achievement.

Working with his speechwriter, we encouraged Doug to reveal elements of his difficult childhood as evidence of his drive to compete. He reluctantly agreed to talk about some of the struggle his family faced. For the first time, he spoke about growing up in a row house outside of Cincinnati, where his parents often went without food so their children could eat. He vividly described unloading trucks and setting up milk cartons at school in exchange for a free breakfast and lunch, as well as how he "graduated" to a summer job at a local steel mill, where he shoved giant hunks of iron into a six-hundred-degree smelter—all of which strengthened his resolve, shaped his worldview, and provided strong incentives never to look back.

By revealing his personal drives, insights, and motivations, Doug was now giving his audience a window into what had shaped his character and why failure was not an option for him. His intention to persuade his salespeople to work even harder and succeed in a challenging market was now much more real and attainable. By sharing very personal stories, Doug touched a common chord. His listeners were inspired. They felt connected, since many had worked their way up from humble beginnings as Doug had. And they were magnetized because Doug's intention was clear and supported by examples of his own personal struggle.

> Let your intention shape your presentation.

As you decide what points of information, stories, anecdotes, metaphors, or examples you want to include, keep asking yourself the question, "Will it lead me toward fulfilling my intention?" Screenwriter William Goldman came up with a basic rule of thumb: "Only put something into your screenplay if it relates directly to the 'spine of the story.'" If you have a great anecdote, but it doesn't relate directly to your intention, lose it. If an entertaining example doesn't propel your intention, lose it. Edit out *all* irrelevancies and streamline your presentation. Look for examples that will achieve your goal. Everything you do should focus on meeting your objective.

Audience-Centered Intentions

In a *BusinessWeek* article titled "How Cisco's CEO Works the Crowd," John Chambers revealed the number-one technique he uses to engage an audience when he speaks. He "sells the benefit"—the dream of a world made better by the company's hardware. His intention is to make people feel better about Cisco rather than to describe the routers and switches Cisco actually sells to link networks and direct traffic over the Internet.

> Everything in your presentation should illustrate and support your intention.

Peter interviewed John Scully, former CEO of both Pepsi and Apple Computers, about what made him a successful speaker. John said he didn't think he *was* a particularly good speaker, but revealed that he leaned on his training in marketing. He always made it a point to find out what audience members wanted from his presentation and then gave it to them.

In an *AARP: The Magazine* article called "Master Class: Fearless Speaking 101," Mario Cuomo (the former governor of New York, who is considered one of our country's outstanding orators) said about audiences, "Know who they are, what they expect to hear, and what they're accustomed to hearing. What's their objective, their purpose in being there? Because that then becomes your purpose. If they've come to learn something about a subject, then you had better be sure to teach it to them."

These outstanding individuals are clear in their intention and masters at directing the focus onto the audience to achieve their own personal results.

> Know what audiences want and give it to them.

However, we advise caution if you strictly follow the dictates of the client or audience too closely. In many instances, our clients were told to come in and introduce themselves or to give a company history during a pitch. If our clients had followed this advice, they would have looked and sounded exactly like their competition. That would not give them the best advantage to win the account. Instead, by having a clear intention, such as "we will demonstrate how we are critical to your success," our clients used *only* the elements of their history and personal résumés that supported this intention. Because in actuality, no matter what potential clients say, they are only concerned with how you can serve them! Think of prospective clients like the old actor's joke: "Enough about me . . . What do *you* think about me?"

COMMUNICATE YOUR INTENTION

Once you have decided on your intention, find a way to make it clear to the audience. Since the strongest position is *not* to state your objective directly, you need to creatively deliver content that drives it. If you are successful, the audience will discover and feel your intention through the congruence of your language, content, and delivery.

Eloqui works with a large biotech firm whose policy dictates that every speaker begins with an "objectives" slide that explains what the attendees should take away (that is, the intention). While this template establishes a clear context for the presentation, it fails to ignite the attentional area of the brain, which is hardwired for novelty and surprise.

Revealing your intention directly can actually dilute the impact of your talk. There is a great deal of research evidence that a message is remembered longer when listeners figure out information for themselves rather than have it spoon-fed to them. This is called *discovery learning*. When you figure out something for yourself instead of being told directly, you better understand the big picture and how it impacts you.

What's My Motivation?

In the theater, when actors are first cast in their roles, they read the script and ask one thing: "What does the character want?" (Of course, this is after they ask, "How big is my part?")

Years ago, I directed the actress Wendie Malick, from the television series "Just Shoot Me," in a short film. Although she's a terrific actress, Wendie was stuck. In the scene, her character's marriage was disintegrating, just as the family was moving into a bigger, more expensive home. Rather than displaying predictable frustration and anger, I directed Wendie to revise her intention. What she now wanted was to return to the time when she and her husband were poor college students and deeply in love, yet knowing it was impossible. A great actress can communicate volumes by a look or gesture, and she did. You could see Wendie's sadness over her husband's inability to change, while *she* had moved on emotionally. As a speaker, you also have more than your words to convey what is important. The first step is to get in touch with your emotions.

My partner David was once cast in the role of Macbeth. His job description was to learn two hours of archaic dialogue and sword-fighting, plumb the depths of avarice and madness, and address the physical requirements of the outdoor theater and audience. Without a clear intention, it would be easy to get derailed.

What is your motivation?

When an actor correctly defines Macbeth's intention as "I want to be king," his job is simplified. Shakespeare never has Macbeth speak this intention aloud, but it is clear from his actions that he is willing to do anything to be king, even commit murder. All of his physical contact with generals is dictated by his intention, as is his fascination with the witches, because he believes they can tell his fortune. Without this clear intention, the audience might be attracted to the actor's line readings, period costumes, changing scenery, and action, but the title character would not be compelling.

I'm Going to Sell You a Car Today!

You are thinking of buying a car. You're interested but still window-shopping. You walk onto a car lot. The salesperson says to you, "I'm going to sell you a car today." What is your gut response? "I don't think so!" Why do you have this immediate negative reaction? The negativity comes from the seller bluntly stating his intention, without including you in the picture. You feel like a mark. It's all about him and what he will gain at your expense.

A better way to achieve his intention would be for the salesperson to say, "What are you looking for in a car?" After your response, he could ask more questions like, "Is resale important to you? What about good gas mileage? Is this car mainly for you, your spouse, and/or your kids?" From your answers, he would then have a good overall picture of your needs,

> Keep your focus on your audience, not on you.

have established a relationship, and would likely achieve his intention, which is to sell you a car. Notice the emphasis is not on the salesman: "I'm going to sell you a car today." It is on you, the audience: "How can I meet your needs?"

Self-Test

Having a clear intention is effective in both professional and personal communications. Whether it's conveying your values, negotiating a business deal, persuading a group to your way of thinking, imparting technical information for training purposes, or inspiring an audience to achieve, the intention makes all the difference.

Reflecting on her movie *A League of Their Own*, the film director Penny Marshall defined each scene as being about one single thing. The scenes were then linked to the overall objective of the film. View it again with this in mind and notice how the intention drove the movie and was a key element in its success.

The next time you have an upcoming talk, write down your intention. Then ask a colleague or two to listen to your presentation and have them tell you what they thought your objective was. See how close they come to identifying it correctly. The closer they are, the clearer your intention. Unfortunately, the opposite is also true.

SELF-DESTRUCTION

If speakers are not careful, they can be at the mercy of negative or destructive intentions. These can include having no intention at all, focusing inward rather than outward (on the audience), or having too many intentions or objectives.

A speaker without a clear intention broadcasts a lack of focus. Minor obstacles become big issues and make speaking difficult, if not impossible. Consider how many times a distraction in the room—such as a computer glitch during a PowerPoint presentation, an audio problem with a PA system, or being told that you have less time than expected—has thrown you off.

All these distractions pale in comparison to focusing on the critic in your head, instead of your one clear intention. Once negative intentions take hold, these are the results:

■ Rushing and cramming in additional material shows the audience that there is no focus or main point to the presentation. It also displays poor organizational skills and an inability to distinguish between important and trivial issues.
■ Displaying little desire to connect with the audience exhibits discomfort and a lack of confidence, even boredom. It makes you look as if you are simply going through the motions of a presentation by rote. To keep presentations fresh, you must commit to your intention.
■ Making the presentation all about you loses your listeners, because they feel unimportant or used. If audience members see you as arrogant and narcissistic, they will not cooperate or support you in achieving your intention.

- Leapfrogging from one topic to another demonstrates a lack of focus and preparation. It can signal too many intentions or no real intention at all.
- Drowning the audience in data diffuses your message and degrades your intention. Limit your data to information that substantiates your intention and supports your point of view.

An audience experiencing a presentation with such elements of negative intention can feel disconnected, bored, and uncomfortable. Conversely, a strong, clear intention at the core of any presentation is the foundation for success. Intention is your safety net. If the presentation is veering off course, remind yourself of your intention, and your delivery will regain clarity and force.

> Commit to your intention.

GOAL SETTING

Intention is one of the more subtle concepts speakers need to identify and employ. Defining your intention is crucial for goal setting. It becomes your scorecard and road map for making future decisions.

■ **Set goals that are directly under your control.** Identify what you can realistically accomplish through your own actions.

■ **Be specific so you can recognize when you have successfully met your goals.** Figure out when you have met each of your objectives by measurable actions. These may include completing tasks you have assigned yourself by specific dates.

For example, if you begin by setting a goal to increase your business 20 percent through networking, you might start with the following: "I will join one networking group within the next month and attend the weekly breakfast meetings as a means of being more visible to potential referral sources. I will also attend one charity event or professional social function per month. At each of these functions, I will deliver a compelling elevator speech or client anecdote when asked, 'so what do you do?'"

Set milestones such as exchanging at least five business cards per event and setting up at least three lunches per month with new contacts you have met at these functions. Then track with your customer database, such as ACT or Excel, how many of these individuals translated into new business opportunities. After six months, eliminate the functions that don't result in direct business or referrals and replace them with new opportunities.

We don't always meet our goals. When you give a talk, it would be unreasonable to expect a standing ovation or multiple requests for your services every time. Setting a goal to do business with everyone in the audience would also not be realistic, because you can't directly control it. You *can* research your listeners' background, demographics, and characteristics; choose a topic that is beneficial to them; and select anecdotal material that supports your intention. This does not guarantee success, but makes it more likely.

Set clear, attainable goals.

Think of intention as the leading edge of a sail: taut and focused. Like the sail that engages the oncoming wind, an intention lifts and drives you to your goal. Your speed and efficiency are based on properly setting your sail or intention. Pick one intention and commit to it. Develop creative ways to express and achieve it. Currents and reefs may provide obstacles, but with a strong intention, you will always reach safe harbor.

2

Roles

As an actor with the Berkeley Repertory Theatre, I was cast as Jason in the Greek play *Medea* but with a twist. The play was to be performed in classical Kabuki style, and Shozo Sato, a former professional Kabuki dancer, was hired as the director. After weeks of learning the demanding vocal and physical style, we were only days away from opening night. At the completion of a three hour full dress rehearsal, I confidently approached the director, panting and sweating, expecting his approval. He said simply, "I didn't see you." I was dumbfounded. I had run the equivalent of a marathon in terms of effort. Sato-san explained that a proper king carried himself with his arms at a precise ninety-degree angle to his body. Mine had drooped ever so slightly, making me invisible and not worthy of attention. A role, whether performed by an actor or a business professional, requires that all aspects be observed and executed with great care. And presenting with others demands an even greater need to be specific and distinct.

A SYMPHONY OF VOICES

Brazilian composer Heiter Villa-Lobos, who was also a cellist, composed a fantasy for orchestra made up exclusively of forty-eight cellos. At first, the piece was engaging because of its odd sound. It may have thrilled other cellists, but after the first few minutes, the lack of variety limited the orchestra's ability to attract and sustain audience interest. Because the cellos had to assume every role in the orchestra, it didn't work.

Each family of instruments has a different role. The basses are the foundation of the music. They play the root of each chord, and their pulse is designed to penetrate your chest. When a composer wants to express a warm, romantic sound, there is the string section with forty violins playing. The winds make the music sound light. Flutes and oboes produce a whimsical tone. When a composer wants intensity, the brass instruments are brought in, and to put it over the top with pounding rhythms, the percussion section is a robust choice. Every instrument performs a vital function in presenting the music to the audience.

Now, imagine a piece of music where the basic pulse was played by the flutes, and the warm, soothing, romantic sounds came from the percussion and brass. Something would feel and sound odd. These instruments would be playing the wrong roles. It might sound comical, but it would not communicate the composer's musical intention.

WHAT IS YOUR ROLE?

To be optimally effective, presenters should always assume a role when they speak, whether in front of a large audience or during a client interaction. Note: I am not advocating *performing* a role, the way an actor plays a character. Rather, the idea is to draw on your experience to choose a business role that will advance your intention. A role will determine how you are viewed.

Roles are also valuable because they direct your focus toward projecting their specific traits, including language, gestures, and behavior. Once you have chosen a role, your attention can shift to your audience or client. Taking the focus off of yourself will reduce your anxiety and self-consciousness. What often trips up speakers is the critical inner voice—"They're judging me, considering how bright I am, how much I know, and how effectively I am communicating." When this voice takes over, a speaker may be unable to think on their feet, resulting in self-conscious delivery.

Mask Theory

Primitive cultures from Mycenaean and African to Native American have all used masks to hide the identity of the wearer and project an archetypal or mythological character. As a student in the theater department at the University of Arizona, we studied the commedia dell'arte of the sixteenth century. Actors used half-masks as a way of suggesting their characters and filled in the voice, mannerisms, and movement. Mask theory is still used in acting academies today to overcome inhibitions and free up the creative juices and expressiveness of young actors.

As a psychologist who specializes in stage fright, it's not surprising that Peter's clientele includes quite a few actors. Most of my fellow performers have no problem with acting a role. They get nervous when they are going to be on TV or live venues as themselves. When actors don't have a role to assume, they feel exposed, and their critical inner voice emerges.

Your role must be congruent with your intention.

One of the keys to successful presentations is selecting a role that is congruent with your intention. Identifying your role as a presenter has three very important purposes: (1) it gives you a clear filter through which to pass information, (2) it helps to ensure that you achieve your intention or goal, and (3) it provides specific guidelines for the language and behavior of that role.

IMPACT

Even a cursory review of research on the psychology of persuasion reveals a major finding for presenters. *Authority is persuasive.* A person will remove their clothing on command if the stranger demanding it carries the authority of a doctor. A person wearing a blue uniform in the role of a police officer can make you move your car or leave the area. We will take the advice of people we don't know well, if they competently assume the role of attorney, accountant, or mechanic (think of the character Doug Rich on the TV series "The Riches," who is a gypsy successfully posing as an attorney without any background or training). Their authority has enormous influence over our decisions. The certainty required to deliver a role projects authority to an audience.

Authority is persuasive.

For example, I played the priest in the opening scene from the film *True Believer* with James Woods. On the set, there were many extras playing the prison inmates, tattooed bikers, and gang members. Except these men were the real thing, and that made the actors more than a little nervous. As I walked around the set, dressed as a Catholic priest, a number of ex-cons came up to me and began to confess their sins or ask for guidance. At first, I vociferously explained that I was only playing a role, but it didn't seem to matter. They still sought forgiveness. I was amazed but realized it was better to stay in the role than tell them they were wrong. All it took was a black suit and shirt and a small white collar.

There are two basic kinds of decision making: emotional and cognitive. We are all familiar with emotional decision making. It's why cars come in different colors and certain products are placed near the cash register. It is also why so many celebrities are hired to endorse products.

Cognitive decisions are different. To make a cognitive decision, you must first do your own exhaustive research, then carefully weigh the alternatives. Most people prefer to have someone they trust do the research and just give them the results. That's why authority plays such a large role in persuasion. Each of the roles in this chapter is designed to project a different type of authority. Choose carefully, because the type of authority your role implies must match the authority that would persuade your audience.

Selection

The major purpose of a role is to fulfill your intention. That is the first thing to consider when selecting your role in a presentation. Your choice is further refined by the role(s) you assume at work and by the characteristics of your audience, even if it's an audience of one.

Professional roles during a presentation can be divided into two categories: big picture and process. The only gray area is the technical expert; someone who has extensive knowledge in an area and is brought in for the express purpose of speaking on a particular subject. Technical expert has limited use in business development, because experts do not typically

> The two categories of roles are big picture and process.

form a connection with an audience/client or invite dialogue. Because of this "stand-alone" quality and requirement for unassailable, comprehensive knowledge, Eloqui seldom recommends that our clients assume the role of expert.

Big Picture and Process

Big picture roles are strategic, provide an overview, and have a perspective from a thousand feet. They include the trusted advisor, the motivator, the mobilizer, the seasoned veteran, and the visionary.

Process roles are concerned with details or the nuts and bolts of an operation, deal, or product. Process roles include the facilitator, the liaison, and the coach. When you are solo, the role that allows you to deliver *both* strategy and detail is the trusted advisor.

Choose a role based on your language and behavior and how you wish to be perceived. For example, Glenn is a portfolio manager with a large investment firm and serves as a trusted advisor to his clients. After knowing their complete financial picture and goals, Glenn makes recommendations for accountants, lawyers, insurance specialists, and other consultants to serve them. He calls on his clients regularly with updates on strategic moves he is making in response to markets and the global economy. Glenn takes into consideration his clients' tolerance for risk, balanced against how many years they have until retirement.

In a client meeting or interaction, Glenn begins with an empathic, warm tone that is congruent with his role as a trusted advisor. This serves to quiet jittery nerves in light of the latest rocky stock market ride. He understands how his clients must be feeling, since he and his wife have invested in some of the same funds. So Glenn suggests strategic changes based on recent research. When questioned, he explains each fund, stock, and bond. However, the details he cites support his overall strategic plan and are presented through the role of a trusted advisor.

Another critical use of selecting a role is to alleviate anxiety and allow you to accomplish your intention, even in a highly charged atmosphere. An Eloqui client from Santa Barbara is one of the foremost dubbing directors in the world. A striking native-born Brazilian, Ariane speaks seven languages and shuttles

> Your role determines your language and behavior.

between Paris, Rome, and Barcelona on a regular basis, as she oversees the dubbing of major Hollywood films. Why would she need to employ a role?

Think of how thin the air gets when a room is populated by, say, Tom Cruise, Steven Spielberg, or other film titans. On one job, Ariane needed more assistants, a larger budget, and less studio interference in order to maintain her level of excellence. So she entered her next meeting in the role of trusted advisor, exhibiting a calm demeanor, empathy, and confidence. When challenged, she gave examples from past projects showing how she organized the talent, maintained the cultural integrity of each language, and made recommendations to ensure that the project came in on time and on budget, successfully delivering the film in eighteen languages. It worked like a charm. Ariane accomplished all of her goals, and her anxiety was held in check.

TEAM PRESENTATION ROLES

What if there is more than one person presenting? How do you decide who fulfills which role? In a two-person or team presentation, division of content and assignment of roles is even more critical. When two partners from a firm meet with a prospective client and lack a clear understanding of their role allocation, they may cover similar ground or speak from the same perspective. For example, if they both only cover strategy, the client may ultimately wonder, "How does this process work?" Without a detail/process person, the two partners have missed an opportunity to express the full range of the firm's capabilities and, more important, may appear to lack substance. The detail or process person conveys the confidence that a company can deliver on its promises.

> Clear division of roles during a team presentation is critical.

Eloqui often sees problems arise when people in the room or pitch do not have a clearly defined role. Van, a managing director for an investment banking firm, and Craig, his vice president, pitched a manufacturing company to sell their business. Van and Craig didn't think about their roles prior to the final pitch (sometimes called a "beauty contest"). During the pitch, Craig deferred to Van, who ran the presentation. At this investment banking firm, it was standard operating procedure to have the managing director take the lion's share of important pitches. So although Craig was present in the pitch, he didn't say much. When they landed the firm as a client, the manufacturing CEO incorrectly assumed that Van would run the day-to-day operations of the deal, because he did most of the talking.

However, process was not Van's strong suit. And it was frustrating for the manufacturing client, who felt the investment banking firm had misrepresented its services and that Van was slacking off, now that the account was secured. In actuality, Craig was responsible for such details, and his skills were crucial to the eventual sale of the manufacturing firm. Craig was the process person and would typically oversee the valuation, assemble and train the manufacturing executives to present the company to potential investors, and construct the timeline to prepare the company for sale.

The frustration for both parties was caused by a breakdown in communication and strategy because Van and Craig did not assign themselves roles during the initial meetings and speak in language specific to those roles. To solve the problem in the next beauty contest, Deborah and I suggested that Van assume the role of trusted advisor and Craig take the role of facilitator or liaison. Craig would actively participate and focus on the details of the transaction, while Van focused on the big picture. Their interaction might sound something like this:

> **Van:** We have seen a 20 percent rise in the value of light manufacturing plants like yours in the last four years, so we think this could be the peak. It's an excellent time to test the waters and potentially put the plant on the market.

Craig: If we're selected, we would begin by having our analysts run the numbers on sales and acquisitions of similar plants throughout Southern California, which we would use as a basis for our projections. We would be in your offices for a week, starting next month, to begin the valuation process, and I will contact you in advance so that you will have the documents and plant ready for that event.

Craig clearly articulates the step-by-step details of the process, showing that he is the one to call when there is a procedural or scheduling question. The client gains a clear idea of each man's function because their roles are well defined. The client will only call Van for strategy questions. Even if Van is contacted with a detail question, the call could easily be handed off to Craig, since his function has also been defined. All of this is reinforced by having each person identify and fulfill his role during the meeting. It not only makes for a successful, persuasive presentation, but it also keeps the client happy in the long run, because roles are clearly understood and all expectations are met.

Establishing clear roles during a presentation has both long- and short-term benefits.

After many years of working with business professionals, Eloqui has identified the roles we see used most often and their primary defining characteristics. Consider these definitions "training wheels" until you are able to adapt the role that best serves your specific objective.

BIG PICTURE ROLES

These roles articulate and frame the overall situation. They deal with information by applying a broad brushstroke. Big picture individuals give comments or advice based on critical acumen, knowledge of a particular industry, and vision. Their perspective comes from considerable experience. Commonly referred to as speaking from the "thousand-foot view," they don't get involved in specifics. It's all concept and strategy. The big picture roles are as follows.

Trusted Advisor

Trusted advisor is the role assumed by most business professionals. However, the term has been misused so often that we believe it necessary to clarify its definition and application. If someone is going to present alone instead of with a team, trusted advisor includes both big picture and detail.

Professionals in the service industry often refer to themselves as trusted advisors. Lawyers; CPAs; insurance brokers; investment specialists; bankers; as well as management, marketing, and public relations consultants are all in positions to develop trust and give advice to their clients. Young people strive to attain this status, which is difficult with a lack of experience.

> The role that includes both big picture and process is the trusted advisor.

A professional will be seen as a trusted advisor if he exhibits the traits of warmth, confidence, empathy, and depth of knowledge. The trusted advisor's role is to provide guidance. He is a good listener and asks probing questions. He serves as a problem solver. In that role he must demonstrate integrity and discretion.

The language of a trusted advisor reflects understanding and concern for the difficulties facing a client. The advisor cites examples of how she solved problems for companies or individuals in similar situations. She frames stories in which her help and advice made a difference. She also demonstrates certainty while acknowledging the inherent complexity or range of choices open to the client.

To shorten the curve of being perceived as a trusted advisor, Eloqui devised the following template and sequence. In this example, we pitched an entertainment law firm in Los Angeles to use our services to create more rainmakers from within the firm and cross market to existing clients.

1. Demonstrate empathy and concern in both your language and tone: "We understand how difficult it is to differentiate your services when there are so many law firms with similar practice groups in the Los Angeles area. And with a number of law firms closing their doors, we appreciate how critical business development is to your survival."
2. Reveal an understanding of the client's challenges and the industry he or she represents: "We know this is a major challenge. As your associates move up the ladder toward partner, they must demonstrate leadership and accrue business development skills to keep the firm healthy and facilitate the senior partners' retirement programs. And we know they may be excellent attorneys, but if your firm is like our other law clients, the associates are not very effective at networking and bringing in new business."
3. Use vocabulary that suggests long-term relationships with other clients: "After training successive waves of associates over the years, we've seen them achieve partner status by exhibiting stronger communication skills, leadership, and business development tools. Many senior partners are now relieved, knowing that the financial well-being of the firms they spent their lives building will be secure."
4. Once trust is established, deliver recommendations or advice: "We recommend that you include communication training early in the associates' curriculum, then revisit and enhance those skills on a quarterly basis to ensure consistent progress and, consequently, the growth of the firm's book of business." If giving direct advice would be considered too forward, tell a story or anecdote to illustrate how you solved a similar problem for another client.

The logic for this order is that trust must first be established through empathy, understanding, and speaking in a way that suggests a long-term relationship. This must be done for subsequent advice to have credibility and weight. Of course, in a real situation, a trusted advisor would ask pointed questions, be a good listener, and make his responses specific to the client to whom he was pitching. He would fold the answers he received back into the conversation.

Application

The trusted advisor template can deliver immediate results. Eloqui recently conducted training for a large toy manufacturing client on the East Coast. Jill, the head of strategic sales was curious to see if she could put the trusted advisor template to work, so she approached William, the director of sales, during a break in the training schedule. She had never been able to engage William in conversation and felt her division suffered as a result, since their teams had to cooperate in presentations.

Jill's impediment was her current position: she had no specific project to work on because she was managing teams, so she felt she had nothing to spark a conversation. That day, while walking on campus, Jill saw William and began with, "It must be difficult to attend management meetings for division heads and then institute all the policies decided upon by corporate." Jill said William was immediately engaged, and they had a lively discussion. She then proceeded through the template and had her first in-depth conversation with him, which ended with him asking her to visit his office for a progress report on her team, which was her intention. She came back to the training session and said, "You won't believe what just happened. This stuff really works!"

In a first meeting or pitch, tell an anecdote relating to the client's issue or concern. Delivering a compelling story of how you solved a similar problem will allow the potential client to identify with the protagonist and put herself in the picture to see how you could best serve her. The story will give the image of you with your shirtsleeves rolled up, actually working in that role. And it will eliminate the need for you to ask for the business.

Embed substantive details in the narrative, instead of listing services like menu items. The perception of a trusted advisor is not based on age, résumé, clients, or service. It is an emotional decision, *supported* by relevant information, only after you have persuaded the client that your services are in her best interest and you are worthy of her trust.

> As a trusted advisor, first establish trust.

Mobilizer

In business, mobilizers are field generals. They focus on the campaign and what it takes to have a successful outcome. They rally personnel, resources, and budget and put them into play to complete the project. Mobilizers have the skill to parlay many disparate services and players at once; they also possess a keen sense of timing, so that all elements coalesce at the given end date. Think of the mobilizer as a "muscle role." If you hear or sense that a client is wondering if your company has the size, scope, or weight to carry a project to completion, employ the language and behavior of a mobilizer, and you will assuage her doubts.

> A mobilizer rallies the troops and keeps his eye on the goal.

Mobilizers require charisma and resourcefulness, and they must demonstrate the leadership qualities of command presence, keen insight, and commitment. They anticipate challenges and, through a positive outlook and force of will, successfully move others forward. Mobilizers are masters of persuasion and exerting influence. They are extremely well organized and able to juggle a number of balls at the same time, while maintaining a strong sense of purpose and focus on the defined outcome.

When presenting, mobilizers are confident that a project will be completed by the agreed-upon date and within the stated budget. They outline the available resources, phases of the time line, any financial restrictions and emphasize the responsibilities of each of the participants. During the course of a project, they hold the vision and keep everyone focused.

Dita, the head of architecture and new build-outs at a Hollywood film studio, was given the assignment of constructing two new office structures within a twelve-month period. She approached her supervisor with a budget forecast that was higher than initially envisioned. Expenditures were an issue at the studio, and her division head pushed back. Dita defended the increase by outlining the specific features that constituted the budget, including broadband access, higher grade insulation, and other technical elements that would deliver long-term benefits for the studio. As a mobilizer, she delivered her game plan for meeting the completion date, as well as the needs of the teams she had in place, with confidence and authority—a sense of command presence. Dita received initial approval and then assembled her teams, from landscapers and electricians to plumbers and building contractors.

Every Monday morning, she brought together the department heads for a progress report. She held each one accountable for their piece of the project. She also stayed on top of each phase to ensure that work was completed on time, inspections were scheduled, permits were obtained, and the next phase begun.

Dita also needed to stay abreast of cost overruns, but she delegated authority for expenditures to the heads of each department. Her leadership qualities and knowledge of the entire process made her effective. Because the mobilizer is a muscle role, it was also Dita's unwavering commitment to achieving the common goal and accountability in overseeing timelines that made her critical to and successful in the process.

Seasoned Veteran

Position yourself as a seasoned veteran when you need to demonstrate perspective and breadth of knowledge in a particular field. The seasoned veteran has fought battles, seen the landscape change over time, and has the ability to predict the future based on history and experience.

One of the many differences between a seasoned veteran and a trusted advisor is that the veteran does not necessarily make recommendations. She describes what she's seen but does not have to be empathic. Because of her direct experience, her opinions have weight, but she doesn't necessarily use these opinions to give advice. Her predictions and assessments of the industry or current climate are valued as indicators of the future and where business is heading. A seasoned veteran can and will say what she believes will happen based on her experience, but it is up to audiences or clients to listen to her opinion and/or change their behavior accordingly.

When I conduct trainings in the corporate arena, I call on my experience as an actor and theater director to position myself as a seasoned veteran. I translate the techniques I taught actors in professional academies like the Pacific Conservatory for the Performing Arts. I use examples of rehearsal challenges, stage blocking, inspiring and motivating the ensemble, and overcoming anxiety as analogues to what business professionals face in their positions.

I compare the considerations of an actor performing a role to what a business professional requires to persuade an audience. This includes intention,

> The seasoned veteran can predict the future based on experience.

focus, and expression of recognizable, authentic qualities. As a seasoned veteran, I cite precedent, demonstrate strength of character, and share survival skills to give my clients a blueprint for success. When presenting with my partner, Deborah, my role of seasoned veteran pairs well with her role as facilitator. She takes my historical perspective, grounds it with logistics and process, and draws out the experiences of the attendees or audience.

Eloqui was working with Bart, a financial wizard who had accomplished his life's dream of traveling to the International Space Station. This achievement garnered him global attention. He wanted to parlay his experience into becoming a positive force on the corporate speaker's circuit, inspiring young people to aim high and achieve their dreams of exploring outer space.

Although Bart has wealth and considerable influence, he described himself as an "amateur actor," who had little skill in the speaking arena and was paid accordingly for his engagements. However, as a former space scientist, he had remarkable analytical ability and a respect for knowledge and experience. Both Bart and I were seasoned veterans in our respective fields.

I began Bart's sessions by delivering an overview of a professional actor's training, the preparation needed before going on stage, and the skills employed during a performance. I cited incidents where a show would have been in danger of falling apart were it not for training and the knowledge of how to respond to a cold audience. To prepare him for the speaker circuit, I told anecdotes of cancelled gigs, bouncing back after poor reviews, and clashes between agents and managers.

I made predictions, based on precedent, that if Bart worked on his skills and speaking tools, he could expect results in a specific time frame. Already a seasoned veteran in the financial arena, Bart felt confident that he could transfer his training to delivering compelling presentations on the speaker circuit. After six months of individual coaching, Bart landed his first paid gig as a keynote speaker at a business retreat for a technology company.

Visionary

Visionaries are inherently idealistic. They paint the possibilities of the future in vivid terms and display foresight, imagination, and certainty. Sometimes their words can possess a lofty, poetic quality. They have to be particularly mindful of reading their audience, for "natural" visionaries can ramble or speak too long. Historically, they have magnetic personalities and are often perceived as great leaders. Think of Martin Luther King, Jr.; Gandhi; and Moses, all of whom articulated compelling visions of the future. Visionaries use words like "I see" or "I imagine." Their general tone is often thoughtful and introspective. But when speaking, they can also become fiery and impassioned, because their message comes from core belief and commitment.

Lewis, the president of a land reclamation company, had to persuade a conservancy organization that his firm would be the best partner for a large development that included sensitive environmental zones and wildlife corridors. He chose the role of visionary to mitigate the potential perception of his firm as a steamrolling, take-no-prisoners land developer. He delivered his talk to the conservancy and local city council, focusing on his vision of the future. He described how this partnership would benefit the city financially while maintaining the integrity of the environment—in essence, being a good neighbor. He vividly described how the homes and retail centers would be adjacent to parks and protected zones so wildlife would not be adversely affected. Lewis delivered his talk with a calm, patient tone that included his belief in how the partnership would be a positive legacy for all of their children and grandchildren. Needless to say, he won approval.

Although visionaries can vividly describe a picture, do not expect them to deliver the details of a project or service. That is the job of a process person. However, to inspire your team, especially if you are in charge, consider selecting the role of visionary. By sharing your perspective and beliefs, and delivering the certainty that the role of visionary demands, you will be persuasive.

Motivator

You have, at some time, probably motivated a friend or loved one to adopt a workout or weight-loss plan. Consider the methods you used when you were successful. There was a definite need expressed—perhaps an upcoming high school reunion, family wedding, or the desire to run a marathon. The goal or objective was clear and attainable. As a motivator, you emphasized the benefits. You were consistently encouraging and excited about the possibilities. You focused on your friend and were enthusiastic in your belief that the outcome was always within reach.

In business, motivators are catalytic agents. They strike the match that ignites the fire. Motivating speakers are inspirational and visionary; they stimulate their listeners to action. Their behavior and language are energetic and positive. Motivators have two mechanisms to employ when persuading their audience: the push and the pull. The push is driving clients by hitting their hot buttons, challenging them, or being persuasive and encouraging. The pull is describing the possibilities so they are inspired to achieve their goal.

> Motivators stimulate their listeners to action.

ROLES: PROCESS

Process roles are the nuts and bolts of a business or service. They are the glue that holds business together. Rather than concentrating on a big picture view, process roles function as the procedural road maps to accomplishing a project. Typically, speakers will assume a process role when they need to convey how something works. They may also choose a process role if they are more comfortable or adept at drawing out the audience, rather than being in the spotlight themselves.

Facilitator

In business, there is an ongoing need for facilitators. They are the greatest ally of the big picture person. Facilitators focus on the detailed view of how projects are accomplished, from arranging meetings and notifying the participants, to scheduling the assignments, drafting an agenda, or when breakfast and/or lunch is delivered. Facilitators tend to ground big picture presenters in reality. They are also the ones to encourage active participation and elicit responses from all parties.

To be perceived as a facilitator, a speaker would confidently walk participants through the look and feel of a process, outlining what everyone is responsible for and specifically what he or she, as the facilitator, will do to assist the procedure.

Because facilitators are dependable, responsible, and hands-on, they are frequently the ones contacted after a deal is concluded to answer specific questions on policy details, time lines, or procedural issues.

> Facilitators ground the vision in reality.

Eloqui was referred to On Point, a custom publishing company in Atlanta that had a do-or-die $5 million pitch looming in the near future. This was an account the company had to win or its business would be crippled and perhaps fold. Its executives were desperate and, as they told us, "drowning in minutiae."

On Point representatives had focused on content—devising flashy PowerPoint visuals and considering production of a video they could ill afford—because they thought it would allow them to compete with their bigger, better-funded competitors. They debated who should take which role and how to convince the client that their company was the best. When we interviewed On Point's presenters, their roles became clear. The president, Davis, was a natural facilitator and gave the presentation a foundation based on his experience and previous interactions with the client. As the facilitator, he could introduce his team members by saying what value each brought to the business process and the presentation. He could detail the objectives of the meeting and how the agenda would break down. While his team presented, Davis could also serve as the eyes and ears of the client, breaking in to clarify a point if he sensed the client was unclear or had a question. As it turned out, Davis *did* direct the presentation and gave it a cohesive structure and flow. Also, by paying close attention to the schedule and participants, his role of facilitator was instrumental in winning the pitch.

Liaison

You have a meeting scheduled with Company X, a midsize information technology firm with sixty employees. The human resources director, Sally, has asked you to come in to discuss insurance coverage for her new hires. As an employee benefits broker, you have access to many different carriers. You are supported by individuals who write policies, research the changing laws, draft employee manuals, conduct training programs, and service claims. When speaking to Sally, you are the connecting point. That is the role of a liaison. Company X is at one end, vital resources at the other, and you are the hub in the center.

Liaisons solve problems, build relationships, and make necessary connections between people. Link all of your dialogue to this image, and you will project this role to your client. Because of their ability to connect and link, liaisons are resourceful, imaginative, and sociable. They form close relationships, know the strengths of all the players involved, and are skilled at handoffs to a specialized source. Their goal is to deliver the correct resources to their clients.

> Liaisons establish connections between people and build relationships.

What you *wouldn't* expect is for a liaison to carry the big picture view. Liaisons don't lead or direct an assignment; they serve and support the effort.

I was having lunch with a colleague recently and was embarrassed because I had never really understood what her services entailed. Mai would typically introduce herself in networking meetings as being in corporate finance, specifically equity and debt placements. This was Greek to me, and without a compelling example, I could not visualize what she did. After working on this section of our book, I realized that Mai was a classic liaison. I tested out this theory the next time I met with her, and sure enough, my assessment was accurate.

Mai explained to me that when a bank turns down a company for financing an acquisition, build-out, or other needs, they come to her. After thirty years, she has established relationships with many lenders and investors. She interviews the company, looks at its structure and earnings, and then brings half a dozen prospects to the table. The match is made, and Mai has fulfilled her role as a liaison. Now that her role was clear, I recommended that she always include client anecdotes when introducing herself, so that others who don't understand her job title can picture her engaged in the process. This clarity will trigger referrals, because as we imagine someone doing business, it sparks our memory of clients who have asked for that specific service.

Choose the role of liaison if you are less experienced but would like to convey that there is a robust company backing you up, if you are in a client pitch but know you won't be directly involved in the actual delivery of services should you win the contract, or if you enjoy connecting people with resources. For example, when you network or socialize to build your business, demonstrate liaison behavior so that those you meet see you as resourceful and a link to their needs. Agents who represent actors, real estate and mortgage brokers, and matchmakers are great liaisons.

Coach

Most people are familiar with the role of a sports coach. The best coaches are great motivators because they understand the specific strengths and weaknesses of each player, but that is only one aspect of their talent and function. Coaches demonstrate leadership qualities such as commitment, belief in their team's ability to excel, and exemplary respect for the rules of competition. They are analytical and critique the performance of their players to achieve the team's overriding objective. Their word holds weight because of their experience and knowledge of the game. The best coaches are respected teachers with a firm sense of resolve. They are goal-oriented and have a game plan to implement, backed up with targeted, detailed actions and knowledge of the players. (Consider John Madden, the retired TV broadcaster and Oakland Raiders' NFL coach who used the "telestrator" to superimpose his hand-drawn diagrams of football plays over live or replay footage so that viewers would better understand the game.)

The role of a coach is similar in business. A coach holds his team accountable. He identifies the potential of and challenges for each participant, provides a training plan, and pushes everyone to succeed. Sometimes a coach's methods may be unorthodox, but he will do whatever it takes to achieve a win for the team and for each player to fulfill his or her potential.

> A coach identifies potential, provides a training plan, and pushes everyone to success.

A Los Angeles–based investment banking firm won a beauty contest and received a contract to sell a manufacturing company called High Performance, which formulates and combines the raw materials that end up as nutritional supplements. One of the founders of the investment banking firm, Adam, brought the deal to the table and decided to shepherd it through. The next step in the process was the "road show." The investment banking firm went on the road with High Performance's management team to face prospective buyers. The investment banking deal team, led by Adam, had to prepare these executives to put their best face forward in order to receive the highest price and best terms.

Adam cast himself as the coach. The coach defines the purpose of the project and makes it about the participants, not himself. Adam assembled the management and deal teams for an initial meeting. He spoke with enthusiasm and resolve. After mapping out his target figure and strategy, he instructed them on the details of how to prepare their approach, speaking points, and presentation structure for the road show. Adam stressed that everything had to be accomplished in two weeks, when their first prospective buyer meeting was scheduled. He encouraged them to focus on their strengths and expressed a vision of success. He sketched out the game plan and motivated the players to believe that the sale could and would be achieved. Like Phil Jackson, coach of the Los Angeles Lakers basketball team, Adam filled the room with conviction and a sense of purpose.

He also brought in outside consultants to refine the presentation skills and handoffs of High Performance's management team. In the meantime, Adam had his analysts review the company's history, profit and loss sheets, and successes and failures; then they prepared an accompanying PowerPoint presentation. He scheduled rehearsals with the entire team and ran through a mock presentation. Afterward, he critiqued the participants' performances and gave them "homework" before the actual pitch.

As the coach, Adam identified each player's strengths and worked with his or her challenges. Adam encouraged the CEO to describe the core values and history of High Performance but to stay on point and avoid his tendency to ramble. In the PowerPoint presentation, Adam instructed the CFO to give the takeaway or most salient point of each financial slide and not go into detail unless asked. He told the sales director to fill in with sales projections in specific markets but to use supportable numbers and real-life anecdotes instead of upbeat generalities. Adam refined and polished the skills of the management team, then rehearsed the investment bankers who would also be presenting. Using motivational language and a corresponding demeanor, he drove them toward projecting that they worked together seamlessly and had a vital and profitable financial future. In the course of the road show, High Performance pitched to eight out of a potential ten companies. They accomplished their goal and exceeded expectations for the sale price.

Technical Expert

When we ask our clients what role they most often assume when communicating with a client or speaking in public, they usually say, "Expert." Unfortunately, when a presenter has chosen the role of technical expert for a presentation, she will do her best to educate rather than persuade her audience. It is not unusual for an expert to include more information than is necessary. We've all endured PowerPoint slides packed with too much text, rambling presentations that go on too long, and speakers' monotone delivery of endless facts and figures. Worse still, it is not surprising to find an expert speaking without considering the needs of her listeners or their response.

Although every role should involve *expertise*, the definition of an expert is someone whose information is irrefutable, inflexible, and highly specialized. Technical experts are typically not people with whom you'd develop long-standing or ongoing business relationships. They are not hired because they are approachable, empathic, or subjective in their assessment. You call in an expert so you don't have to read the manual. An expert is your substitute for detailed instructions.

Not only does choosing the role of technical expert put an inordinate amount of pressure on the speaker, but achieving expert status is usually unrealistic and, more important, an ineffective means of achieving buy-in. There are appropriate venues for technical experts, but they tend to be limited to brief stints that support a more persuasive presentation when a propeller head, an analyst, or a technician is required.

Rarely do we advise selecting the technical expert as the most effective role in business interactions, presentations, or networking. Since an expert is basically unapproachable and is usually expected to have in-depth knowledge of a particular subject, the role is primarily useful in conjunction with other presenters when a detailed analysis or assessment of a sector or industry is required. In this instance, delivering analytical or statistical data in support of another speaker is the proper role for an expert. Experts are best as complements to team leaders but rarely should lead a presentation or client meeting.

If you must fill the role of a technical expert (such as on the witness stand or in a client pitch), here are a few things to consider. An expert is committed and certain and speaks in quantitative, absolute terms. An expert has no trouble substantiating his findings. If you choose the role of expert, do not use qualifying terms like "maybe," "potentially," or "I think." Instead, use phrases such as "I know . . . ," "The facts are . . . ," or "These statistics indicate that . . . ." Also, do not include emotional or value statements. Experts don't make recommendations, collaborate with their listeners, or motivate their audiences. You expect an expert to deliver well-researched information and their findings in a straightforward manner with no subjectivity or emotion.

> Technical experts should be cast *only* in supporting roles.

To put the role of expert into perspective, remember this simple axiom: If you educate us, you get us to think. But if you persuade us, you get us to act.

SELECTING A ROLE

Once you've determined what you want to achieve with your presentation, the next step is to select the role that best drives that intention. After you decide how you want to be perceived, the task of selecting your role becomes easier. Here are a few examples:

- To close a deal and show a potential client your firm's ability to get a job done on time and on budget, the mobilizer role has the right muscle.
- To incentivize your client to submit paperwork by a certain date, the role of motivator may be most advantageous.
- To be seen as the conduit to fund-raising resources for a nonprofit client, the role of liaison may be appropriate.

The role you choose is determined not only by your intention, but by your audience and the forum where you are presenting. In your work, you assume different roles at different times, depending on what you would like to achieve during that event or interaction. You may be a coach when counseling a younger associate, a visionary when branding your services, a trusted advisor when it comes time to close a deal, and a motivator when encouraging your staff to perform better.

In the course of a day, you naturally select the proper role for the situation you find yourself in. It seems obvious that if you are rolling out a new product and play a role in marketing, you would refine that role based on your intention, so you might be a mobilizer or coach. But the situation isn't always so clear. What if you have an underachieving employee? As a manager, is it better to assume the role of motivator or trusted advisor? The situation, the employee, and your expertise all influence your selection of the appropriate role. You have a similar choice as you prepare for a presentation.

Select the proper role to use in your presentation. Select *only one* for maximum effect. Shifting between two or more roles will result in a loss of focus for both you and the audience. It can cause you to ramble and confuse your listeners. Another advantage of choosing just one role is that you are relieved of the responsibility of doing more than that role requires.

> Choose one role and perform it well.

Selecting and presenting through a role is not an acting exercise where you portray a character. Choose a role directly from your experience. Play to your strengths. Your role should be as familiar to you as the route you take to work each day. The selection of a role is actually a narrowing down of the many choices you have to the one that will most effectively engage your audience and achieve your intention. A role defines who you are and what you want to deliver. It sharpens your intention and focuses your content. The alignment of intention and role sharpens your presentation, which satisfies your audience or client.

How do you know if you delivered an identifiable role to your audience or client? One metric is the type of questions and comments you receive after a presentation. For example, if you assume the role of an expert, expect questions regarding data analysis, technical features, or projections. In contrast, if you assume the role of a trusted advisor, the questions will focus on what you would recommend in a specific situation. And when you present as a seasoned veteran, expect questions about where the industry is headed or the implications of past events.

Rules of Roles

- From the first spoken word, your language and behavior must be congruent with the role you assume.
- Choose only *one* role and exhibit its characteristics throughout your entire presentation.
- Fully commit to the role and do not "break character" during the presentation.
- Every role requires expertise, but we strenuously suggest that you avoid assuming the role of technical expert unless you are an expert witness or analyst in a firm where you are focused on the science or in-depth analysis of a subject.

Aristotle called Ethos one of the three essential elements of speaking. Ethos is defined as the state of being, the inner source, the soul, the mind, and the original essence that shapes and forms a person. Pulling that essence from your inner being and giving it form with a role will identify you and make you compelling. Select a role and keep it consistent to engineer the perception you most wish to create. And remember my Kabuki example: make your behavior and language congruent, lift your elbows as the king, and you will never be invisible.

3

Premiere

How to Open

For months, you've been looking forward to attending the theater and seeing an avant-garde production of a much-publicized play. You've paid a small ransom for tickets, driven an hour on the freeway, wedged your car into a crowded parking deck, and inhaled dinner to arrive on time. You're sitting expectantly in the audience of the Ahmanson Theatre in downtown Los Angeles. It's 8:00 P.M. The lights dim.

A lone actor walks on stage and says, "Good evening, ladies and gentlemen. I'd like to thank the Ahmanson board of directors for providing this wonderful space for tonight's program. Speaking of tonight's performance, I am pleased to announce you will be treated to 120 minutes of gripping theater, consisting of three acts. The play is titled *Shades of Aubergine* and was written by MTV director Dirk Terabyte. *Shades of Aubergine* will cover birth, death, marriage, madness, and infidelity. And oh, by the way, in the third act, the hero dies. At the conclusion of the play, please join the actors for a thirty-minute Q&A session. Thank you for being with us. I hope you enjoy tonight's performance."

If actors delivered introductions like this, we would quickly witness the death of theater as we know it. Without surprise, expectancy, and the ability to transport ourselves into another world, there is no engagement. And without vivid characters, creative sets and costumes, witty dialogue, and a compelling story, the mystery would be gone and so would our interest.

Steven Johnson, author of *Mind Wide Open*, says, "The brain's attentional and memory systems are designed to record novelty and surprise." Researchers now believe that there is an entire neurochemical system in the brain devoted to the pursuit and recognition of new experiences. Yet we ignore these findings when it comes to business presentations. The formality of old business models leads professionals to lay out every detail in advance, eliminating all possibility of novelty or surprise.

> Our brains are hardwired to pay attention to novelty and surprise.

OPENINGS

After reading the following three openings to presentations, try to recall specific details and what is novel about each construction.

Opening 1

Good morning. My name is Martha Weintraub, and I'm with Johnson Farwell. We're financial advisors who work with high–net worth individuals to help our clients maintain their wealth by solving the problems that keep them up at night. We care about our clients and give them our cell numbers so they can reach us 24/7. Over the next thirty minutes, I will present creative investment options that will allow you to achieve your retirement dreams.

Opening 2

Ladies and gentlemen of the Winthrop Banking Association. I want to thank you for your gracious invitation to have me speak at your annual meeting on membership participation. I have been with the Association for more than twelve years and have considered it a privilege to be a member. Before I begin, I would like to thank President Markis and our esteemed treasurer, Joe Turner. And of course, I would like to thank all of you for taking time out of your busy schedules to attend. On my way to the meeting, I thought of a funny story that I'd like to share . . .

Opening 3

My name is Mark Bernstein. I am president of the special community we call Congregation Isaiah Israel. It is an honor and a privilege to welcome you to our High Holy Day services this year. As I look out at the congregation, I see many familiar faces. Some of you may be new to our congregation, new to the community, or just visiting. For those who are with us for the first time, please be assured that the members of our congregation welcome you as family.

Our Rankings

If you couldn't remember many details or determine much difference between the three examples, Eloqui wholeheartedly agrees. On the positive side, the openings would not offend anyone in the audience. But they immediately telegraph that the rest of the presentation will be traditional, predictable, and tedious. Why? Although polite and gracious, each of these openings lacks specific details, relies on phrases we've heard many times before, and is missing the speaker's personal insight or perspective. They do little to engage the listener. They represent the opposite of novelty and surprise. And none of them are driven by a singular objective.

These openings also lack authenticity. People don't talk like this. Imagine if your administrative assistant came into your office and said, "I'm here to talk to you today about whether you would like regular or decaf and the various options of low-fat, nonfat, whip, or soy. Over the course of the next two minutes, I will go over the benefits of each so that you will be able to make an informed decision." You would probably think he had lost his mind.

Too often, business presentations begin with a perfunctory "thank you," followed by a "glad to be here," and then spell out a detailed agenda with the main points or overview of the upcoming talk. There is no originality, heightened expectation, or surprise. The old models of formality rule. Notice the speaking voice that accompanies these traditional openings. Typically, it will sound flat and lifeless because the speaker has assumed a professional business mode and is boring even herself. The worst offense is that the audience is not engaged during the critical first few minutes and they hold out little hope that the rest of the presentation will be any better. You *can* make your opening more dynamic, vital, and, ultimately, persuasive.

> A boring opening signals a boring presentation.

DIVE OFF A CLIFF

Create a powerful framework in your opening so that the remaining content will be delivered within the frame you've constructed. In the following examples, notice how the speaker jumps right in and dives off a verbal cliff instead of beginning with predictable introductions or "windups" (fillers).

■ **Counterintuitive questions.** "China has a history of disregarding copyrights. Of all the products whose copyrights are infringed, where do you think the most violations are found?" Pause and solicit a few responses. The answers most people give are movies or CDs. "The number-one copyright infringement in China involves Prozac."

From this opening, you can segue to legal issues, trade, or the prevalence of depression, but the important thing is you've grabbed your audience's attention. You've also signaled that you have proprietary or confidential information. Having discovered this, the audience will want to hear more.

■ **Attention-getting statements.** "Attractive people are more persuasive than average-looking people. How does this affect your business?" From this opening, you can discuss ways to level the playing field, various aspects of persuasive speaking, or ways to generate new business. You may even address how the public votes for the most attractive candidate in a political race. What you've done is make audience members think about how *they* fit into the attractiveness spectrum, and by doing so, you will have engaged them.

■ **Personalization.** Tell a personal anecdote where you demonstrate why you are passionate about your subject or reveal your values. "My high school science teacher reminded me of Albert Einstein. His hair stuck out from his head in spiky clumps, he spoke in rapid-fire sentences, and he paced around the room when he lectured. One day, Mr. Edwards came in to our physics class with a huge green trunk and plopped it in down in front of my bench. Inside was a jumble of tubes, wires, and parts. It was World War II radar equipment, and he said, "Make it work, Gordon." It looked impossible, but Mr. Edwards had a way of pulling the best out of people. So I made it happen.

"From there, I started my own ham radio station. In college, I majored in electrical engineering. And at Gendyne, I ran a division of three thousand people who made microcircuits. Here at Sun Electro, your world is exploding. This reorganization may look like the jumble of wires and parts in Mr. Edwards's trunk. Know that I will be here to guide you through the process. And eventually, you too will make it work."

There is abundant evidence that we prefer listening to examples and stories rather than being lectured at. We also tend to believe anecdotal evidence over facts and figures.

HONEYMOON PERIOD

As a speaker, you have a honeymoon period that lasts from thirty to sixty seconds. In less than a minute, you must grab your listeners' attention and make them want to hear what you have to say, or they will determine you are not worth listening to and relegate you to the dustbin of "dull and predictable." The research on viewer behavior with a remote control indicates that TV programs have the same brief amount of time to capture our attention.

Web developers have coined the term "sticky sites," which refers to websites that make you want to linger and look around, as opposed to clicking to go somewhere else. Your audience may be forced to sit in front of you, but if you don't have a "sticky" opening, people can click the button on their cerebral cortex and switch to anything else that is more engaging, which includes their Blackberry, laptop, and imagination.

> You have between thirty and sixty seconds to grab your listeners' attention and prove to them that you are worth listening to.

When you begin a presentation with expressions such as "I'd like to introduce . . ." or "I'm going to talk about . . ." or "I'd like to welcome you all to . . . ," you are using windups. Since you are obviously introducing, talking, or welcoming, such phrases are redundant. They create distance between you and your audience instead of delivering striking visual images that force your listeners to pay close attention.

Windups are mechanisms to fill the void before addressing the substance of your presentation. But they're not the only offenders.

Linguists call repeatable words or phrases that substitute for a pause "discourse particles." They include "you know," "um," and "just." Like windups, discourse particles are buffers that speakers employ when thinking or formulating an opinion. In either case, jumping into the subject directly or using a pause is much more effective.

TARGET YOUR AUDIENCE

Speakers use generic openings to be inclusive of the various personalities and cultural backgrounds in the room. The outmoded belief is that by being general, you are polite and demonstrate respect for heterogeneous audiences. In actuality, the reverse is true. To be universal, you must focus on one personal experience, story, concept, or idea. Without specific details, a speaker does not truly connect with *anyone*. However, if you use salient details and relate your own experience or point of view, listeners will process your content through the filter of their own experience. An original opening engages and orients your audience, lighting up the attentional and memory centers in the brain.

> Without specific details, you won't connect with your audience.

Communication psychologist Mark Leary points out the importance of engaging an audience right away. He recommends three things to consider in your opening:

1. **Tailor your talk to the audience.** Signaling that you understand the needs, perspectives, and/or expectations of your listeners lets you target what interests them and select the most compelling stories, anecdotes, and examples.

2. **Reveal your personal values.** Share what motivates or inspires you to move audience members and get them involved. Even though they may not agree, you have provided a revealing

window into your thinking. Persuasion and influence are now more likely, because your listeners believe they know you.

3. Present your point of view on the subject. Revealing your perspective allows your audience to understand your intention, context, and passion.

Picture your listeners holding remote controls or mouse in their hands as you begin your talk; your goal is to keep them from flipping the channel or clicking through to another page. Following are two client examples of nontraditional, dynamic, and personal openings:

> In hockey, there's a two-foot gap between your kneepads and shorts where you expose a big portion of your thighs. It's called a "geek gap." I was tall, skinny, couldn't skate very fast, and played second string on the high school junior varsity hockey team. I had a really big geek gap. This meant getting bruised a lot. So I dropped down to the third-string team, played center, and became the high scorer against players who couldn't exploit the gap as much. Yexa Technology used to play in the PC market, and we had a very big geek gap. So we dropped into the thin client market, and now we're number one. If this resonates with your challenge, consider dropping down a level, reducing the geek gap, and becoming number one in your market space.

Notice how this opening jump-starts the imagination. When you present specific details, listeners participate mentally and visualize your story, even though it's not about them. When you read the example, what went through your mind? Did you recall a similar challenge or setback in your own childhood or adolescence? If you did, you're like most audiences. We can't help but identify and relate everything to our own experience.

Also, the term "geek gap" is funny and colorful. It hits a universal point of interest—vulnerability. It sets up potential clients to examine their own weaknesses and look for solutions for dealing with them.

Following is the opening the congregation president, Mark Bernstein, actually delivered on Yom Kippur, instead of the third example given at the beginning of this chapter.

> In 1994, my son, Bredon, was born. My wife, Dianne, and I immediately recognized something was different about this child. His head was misshapen, and he lacked motor control. A parade of specialists delivered prognoses of doom and gloom, and a deep fog settled on us.
>
> Months later, as the High Holy Days approached, I was prepared to go to the synagogue and ask God why he had given us a child who was supposed to be perfect yet had so many disabilities.
>
> I awoke one morning to Dianne's smiling face. She said, "Mark, I finally realized that Bredon didn't happen *to* us. Bredon happened *for* us." At that point, I realized that Bredon was God's gift. It is just that this gift arrived in an unexpected package.

There was no windup, no fat or wasted words. The congregation immediately connected with Mark's tone, his theme, and his very personal investment in the subject matter. Even though the members may not have experienced a child of their own having birth defects, they were launched on the narrative journey with the speaker—all in about one minute. It was a beautiful opening to a memorable speech about accepting what you are given and making the most of your opportunities.

PRIMACY AND RECENCY

For well over a century, psychologists have stressed how well we remember the first and last things we hear. Whether it's recalling items on a shopping list or in your presentation, people tend to remember the beginning and the end most easily. Your opening orients your audience to who you are and sets the tone for what will follow. The next chapter deals with effective methods for closing.

Your Order Please

The principle of primacy is based on the idea that the first items you are presented with are learned better and retained more easily because they are less likely to be interfered with by other items. This makes them stand out. Interference is considered the major cause of forgetting. Similarly, the principle of recency works because of the same reason. Because nothing else follows the items at the end, there is less opportunity for interference.

When you present information in a sequence and the order is important, such as in a series of instructions, then the items at the beginning are retained well. When the order does not matter, the items at the end are recalled more easily. In either case, however, the information in the middle is always the most difficult to recall. Use the principle of primacy to place important information that will guide the audience into the rest of the presentation at the beginning. Use the principle of recency to place the most important information at the end, because this is what you want people to remember.

ELEPHANT IN THE ROOM

If a problem or concern is affecting your client or audience, don't bury it. Since a concern is always foremost in people's minds, they will wonder when you will address the issue or will be irritated that you are seemingly avoiding it. In either case, they will not pay attention to anything else you talk about. Speak about the concern first to defuse a potentially volatile situation. By addressing "the elephant in the room," you display courage and consideration.

When Arnold Schwarzenegger was running for governor of California, a news item alleging that he groped women broke prior to the election. Rather than ignoring or denying it, Arnold held a press conference and apologized for any misbehavior in his youthful past. He stressed how much he admired and respected women. Playing the vulnerability card, he said any damage he may have done was purely unintentional. Arnold derailed the issue by facing it head-on.

In the 2002 film *8 Mile*, Eminem's character is facing public humiliation and the end of his budding career as a rapper. Pitted against the popular favorite Papa Doc, Eminem's character takes the stage first. Instead of trying to out-rhyme and outperform his rival, he electrifies the room by grabbing the elephant. Using self-effacing humor, Eminem mocks his own life—from living in a trailer with his mother to losing his girlfriend to his rival. Because he has stolen all of Papa Doc's ammunition and material, he becomes the uncontested favorite and wins the competition.

SENSORY CINEMA

The goal of your opening is to get your listeners to play—and later replay—a movie scene in their heads. You can do this by giving them images that are emotional and rich in detail. Make this movie something they can relate to. Evoke sensory images. Which of the following two sentences is more evocative?

- At the beginning of 2000, emerging companies had a difficult time raising money.
- Emerging companies were the piñatas of venture capitalists during the tech wreck.

In terms of information, these statements are equivalent, but in terms of imagery, they are miles apart. The metaphor of a piñata evokes bashing an object, kids screaming, and the thud of the stick against a vibrant, papier-mâché chicken. It provides the listener with a visual snapshot linked to your idea.

Sensory details are key to a good opening.

You can also tap into emotions through personal identification. A colleague, Denise, who opened a Women Who Mean Business awards ceremony evoked a visceral response from the audience. Her story resonated with many of the women in the room:

> Seven years ago, my husband and I divorced. We had been together for twenty years. My husband was also my business partner in a custom software firm. My mother also died that year; in times of crisis, she had been the person I always turned to. As a young widow with four children, she taught me to be resilient and positive, no matter what life throws at you. And then, I swear this is not a country-western song, my dogs died. I was challenged to find new footing. If ever there was an opportunity and a need to reinvent myself, this was it.
>
> According to the U.S. Department of Labor Statistics, the average person makes more than three career changes during his or her working life. This was about number seven for me. Sometimes you reinvent yourself by choice, particularly in an economy where industries and businesses are in flux—or if you are divorcing your business partner. Sometimes circumstances require you to reinvent yourself.

OPENING TRIGGERS

Earlier, we listed three methods for crafting a unique opening: counterintuitive questions, attention-getting statements, and personalization. Eloqui has devised opening triggers to stimulate your imagination so that you can develop your own creative openings.

These triggers are hooks or jumping-off points to engage your audience. To be effective, they must be brief and link quickly and thoughtfully to your topic. They are preludes and are not intended to stand alone. You don't want your audience wondering why you are telling a story or anecdote that does not directly relate to your topic. The next time you have a presentation, elevator speech, or pitch, choose one of the following opening triggers and use it to frame your material.

> An opening trigger will stimulate your audience's imagination and make listeners more attentive.

- Identify a role model who had a major influence on your life. How has this person affected your values or operating principles?
- Use a strong metaphor or simile that gives your audience a vivid image of your business or presentation topic.
- Explain how moving to your current location or away from your hometown has affected you.
- Describe a childhood event that had a major effect on you or was a catalyst for your choice of profession.
- Choose a sport or competitive event that you participated in and relate the lessons you learned.
- Recall a setback or disappointment that turned out to have a positive outcome.
- Pick a current event with an emotional charge from the headlines and relate it to your subject.
- Think of a life-changing event and how it has influenced you.
- Select a favorite movie, book, or play and relate the characters, story line, or theme to your topic.
- Recall what your parents wanted you to become and how that impacted you.

MEAT ON THE BONE

Once you have selected an appropriate trigger, flesh out a more robust opening.

▪ **Use visual imagery to engage the audience's imagination.** Rather than saying you're a realtor who deals in high-end property, make your description more specific and colorful; for example, "Drive down Camden Avenue between Sunset and Santa Monica, and you'll see more than ten houses I've sold."

▪ **Add graphic similes or metaphors.** People relate to comparisons that stimulate their imaginations.
  □ After an avalanche, a representative from a Colorado ski resort said the conditions were like "trying to park a Cadillac on top of a pile of potato chips."
  □ A scientist with the Human Genome Project said, "Cells are a recombinant form, which is why the same twenty to twenty five thousand cells can become a giraffe or a human. It's like three authors using the same dictionary and creating three entirely different novels."
  □ Either James Watson or Francis Crick compared the motion of the genetic replication process to a tightrope walker. Each time the performer steps forward, a new DNA strand is formed under her foot.

▪ **Avoid lengthy openings.** Compress and edit your opening so that it consists only of the most essential details. The opening is meant to set the tone and frame your content. Don't make it so compelling and long that it becomes the focus of your presentation. Most openings can be delivered in less than two minutes.

▪ **Appeal to the five senses.** In addition to visual images, on occasion include taste, smell, sound, or touch.

■ **Create segues to transition quickly from the opening trigger to the subject matter of the presentation.** The earlier geek gap example illustrated how to make a smooth transition from an opening story to the main point of the presentation about finding your position in the marketplace. The key here is *relevance*. The best opening trigger piques the imagination and then makes an intelligent link to your topic.

COME FROM STRENGTH

A well-crafted opening displays creative thinking. By relating stories or insights from your own experience, you take the opportunity to reveal your unique perspective. Using your own experience also adds confidence to your opening. There is abundant psychological research showing that speakers experience the most anxiety in the few minutes before and the first two minutes during a presentation. Speaking about something that is familiar to you reduces this anxiety and keeps you from losing your place or freezing up.

Always play to your strengths.

In addition, when you play to your strengths and speak from your experience, you will be more animated and persuasive. An audience or a client will respond more positively, because you bring your personality and knowledge to the presentation.

BIRTH OF A THEME

The other advantage of a well-crafted opening is that it will usually suggest a theme to be revisited throughout your presentation. A theme is an easily repeatable phrase or thought that encapsulates the essence of your message. Think of it as the central idea. In music, a theme is defined as a principal, recurring melody intended to convey a mood. Ideally, when you are speaking, a theme should firmly implant an idea or point of view in your listener's memory. The following are a few examples of memorable themes:

Just do it!
We adapted, improvised, and overcame.
Gift your children, not the IRS.
It's the economy, stupid.
It's for the kids.
Hold your ground.
Life is not a static event; protect yourself.
It's either right or wrong.

Easily repeated themes are fixed in the listener's long-term memory. They can be employed to build momentum, to reinforce your body of evidence, or to persuade your audience to take action. As in music, a variation on a theme keeps it alive and vibrant. Different instruments, varying tempos, and a change in volume all illuminate the theme. In speaking, themes can serve as a transition between sections or allow a speaker to conclude and pay off a concept in a vivid and compelling style.

In the congregation president's Yom Kippur opening, the theme was "Gifts come in unexpected packages." Throughout the remainder of Mark's talk, he described how his son's disability became a "gift" to members of his family. And as each new section of his presentation was introduced, it was knit together by this theme, building to his conclusion, adding weight and integrity to the overall presentation.

> A theme is defined as a principal, recurring melody intended to convey a mood or central idea.

For example, in the body of Mark's talk, he described how his daughter's desire to teach Bredon communication skills motivated her decision to become a speech therapist. Because of Bredon's gift, Dianne refocused her law practice from civil litigation to special education law, representing families of children with disabilities. And the family formed a nonprofit organization that raised $2 million to create a playground for special needs children.

ANALYZE YOUR AUDIENCE

An audience analysis is one tool you can use to prepare for your presentation, so that your opening—and the entire talk—will be tailored to your audience. This information will also be key in determining your intention (what you wish to achieve), framing your content, and choosing your role. Obtain relevant demographics, and do your best to answer the following questions:

- How many people will attend my presentation?
- What is the average age, and is there a large range?
- Where does the audience fit on the organizational chart (for example, are they high-ranking decision makers, middle management, or technical staff)?
- What is the corporate culture? In the past, IBM executives were expected to wear dark suits, white shirts, and dark ties. Their presentation style was similarly formal and structured. Now there are businesses where even the CEO dresses casually. As a speaker, match your dress and tone to the corporate culture.
- Is the industry relatively conservative (like investment banking) or more expressive and loose (like video gaming or Internet marketing)?

The best way to ferret out this information is to know someone on the inside. If you do not have access to such a person, research the company on the Internet or in newspapers and journals. Talk to colleagues who may have made presentations before you. Get as much detail as you can. It will be vital in shaping your content and delivery, especially your opening.

VERBAL CALLING CARDS

Elevator speeches are special occasions when your opening *is* your presentation. Such a speech gives a short introduction about you, your services, and your company—in short, a verbal calling card. Picture being in an elevator with someone you would like to impress and having only the duration of the ride in which to do it.

When you find yourself with an opportunity to make a quick introduction to a key individual or group—be ready. Do it in an interesting and memorable way. Imagine you met someone in an elevator and he said, "Hi, my name is George Henderson, and I sell group medical insurance. Here's my card. Call me if I can ever help you." Chances are you would toss his card into the nearest trash receptacle.

Instead, think about what would happen if you asked George what he did and he told you the following: "At Buellton Insurance, we were able to cut a client's group medical costs by 40 percent. We analyzed the numbers and used our influence with carriers. The best part was that they didn't sacrifice any benefits."

Although this second version is better, it still lacks personalization. Crafting brief elevator speeches from your personal experience and including vivid details and differentiators is difficult. As Mark Twain said, "I didn't have time to write a short letter."

> Have a memorable "calling card."

Following are a few examples of elevator speeches from Eloqui clients. Note how the best ones include the speakers' personal traits to set them apart, as well as visual details of how they function. Depending on the venue, you have between thirty seconds and two minutes to deliver an elevator speech.

I played goalie on a Canadian hockey team. I relished the heat and challenge of the game. Now, as an audit CPA, I represent law firms and protect them by deflecting blistering slap shots from the IRS and defending against possible embezzlers. And I must be good, because I still have all my teeth. [Big smile.]

Wine is about chemistry. You need quality grapes that are picked at the right time. You have to weed out seeds and stems and add yeast and sugar to ultimately make a wine that is harmonious. This is what creates a great experience. If you try and save a few bucks, you get wine in a box, which you'd better drink soon or it will turn to vinegar.

With business, you also need the right chemistry and experience. When people show up at my door considering bankruptcy, I know the chemistry wasn't right, key ingredients were missing, or they made poor decisions. But that doesn't mean their business was a total failure. Downturns happen. And sometimes it's beyond their control. So I salvage what I can—before it turns to vinegar. I'm John Williams, and I provide economic solutions to struggling companies and individuals as a bankruptcy attorney.

Bruce and Irene thought they had enough to retire. But they overlooked taxes, inflation, and living past the average life expectancy. As their financial advisor, I recommended they turn their hobbies into revenue streams. Now Irene's quilts are in local galleries, and Bruce sells his refinished furniture on eBay.

Have you ever had this happen to you? Spending four to six hours at a dealership trying to get the car *you* want but walking away with what *they* chose for you? Trying to leave the lot but being turned over to another salesman? Paying more than you should have for accessories? Being frustrated shopping for a car and not wanting to ever go through the process or walk onto a dealership lot again? I'm Robert Chavez, a personal auto broker who takes the hassle out of car shopping and makes sure you get exactly the car you want at a fair price.

Like any presentation, analyzing your audience before crafting your elevator speech will give you a leg up on achieving your goal.

Know your audience!

For example, if you are the guest of a Century City business group in Los Angeles that is comprised of mostly entertainment lawyers and accountants, choosing an emotional, personal elevator speech may not be your best option. Relating a current news event to your business, especially one that focuses on the entertainment industry, would be wiser.

On the other hand, if you are presenting to human resource directors who tend to be more idealistic in nature, include an example that emphasizes your connection to your clients, how your business contributes to the greater good, or why you are passionate about what you do.

Fundamentally, it is impossible and never recommended to include everything you do in one elevator speech. Attempting to do so with umbrella statements will inevitably lead to generic descriptions that fail to resonate with anyone. Instead, pick one message and give vivid examples to support it. Then, if you have the opportunity to speak to the same group again, pick another message or aspect of your business to focus on. Over time, your audience will form a composite of who you are and what your company does. You can always wrap your firm's full range of services into a concluding

People do business with individuals they know and trust. Make sure your audience knows you.

summation or tag line. For example, an intellectual property attorney might conclude his elevator speech this way: "In addition to protecting our entertainment clients' intellectual properties, our firm also provides environmental, estate planning, transaction, and real estate services."

Our clients have expressed concern that if they give an example that doesn't apply to someone in the room, they have lost the possibility of doing business with that person. In truth, if you are compelling with each of your elevator speeches, you have given listeners a window into your perspective and values so they feel as if they know you, which can be far more important. Since people do business with individuals they know, trust, and like, if you have made a positive connection, you will probably be asked about the other services your firm provides that you didn't include in your introduction.

To be memorable, Eloqui recommends *not* leading off with your name and business. We know this may sound heretical and is counter to the traditional model for introductions, but our experience says there is a more effective way. When you give your name and business up front, two things are likely to happen. First, if your listeners have a preconceived notion of insurance brokers, lawyers, or accountants, they will drop you into that slot. Don't allow them to decide that you are like every other insurance broker, lawyer, or accountant they know. Or, if they don't need the services that your business provides, they could decide not to listen to the rest of your elevator speech. Second, audience members do not yet have a visual image or context to associate with you. Because they need a marker to put you into long-term memory, the likelihood is they won't remember you or your business.

> Don't lead off with your name and business.

On the positive side, if you start with an engaging story, visual, or framing device and *then* give your name and business, it is much more likely that they will remember you. For an added boost, you can repeat your name at the end of your elevator speech. Repetition, used sparingly, is a good way to assist the process of transferring information into your listeners' long-term memory. As noted earlier, the principle of recency says we tend to remember the last thing we hear.

Elevator speeches need to be brief and colorful and, when appropriate, end with a tagline that summarizes your unique personality and/or business or services. The idea is to lock what you do in the minds of your listeners and give them an easily repeatable description that distinguishes you.

NEVER BEGIN WITH AN APOLOGY

Because the number-one fear in America is public speaking, many speakers choose to deal with anxiety by lowering the audience's expectation with an apology such as the following:

- ■ "I'm not really an expert on this subject, but I'll give it a go."
- ■ "Forgive me, but I'm a little nervous tonight."
- ■ "I've only been in this job a few months, but . . ."
- ■ "I didn't expect to win, so I didn't write anything."

Apologies don't work. The rationale for using this strategy is that when you say you're nervous and then don't do too badly, the audience will have expected very little and then praise you for how well you did. People may even have a little sympathy for you. However, as Peter has written in his books on stage fright, an audience that pities you will not respect you.

Even worse, when you tell listeners you're nervous, you're directing them to search for visible signs of anxiety. You are, in effect, telling them to notice if your hands or legs are trembling, you're sweating excessively, or your voice is shaking. If they are going to discover your nervous state, let them do it on their own—don't focus attention on it. Audiences rarely notice such things unless they are dramatically obvious. If your hands shake, don't hold a piece of paper to accentuate it. Psychologist Arnold Buss pointed out that anxiety symptoms always appear much more pronounced to the speaker than to the audience.

Always present with authority.

If you tell your listeners you are not an expert, they will resent the fact that an amateur is taking up their valuable time and will look for evidence to confirm your lightweight status. This is not a good strategy for being taken seriously. Imagine your surgeon saying to you prior to an operation, "I'm not real good at this type of surgical technique, so just bear with me. Oh, and I tend to get a little nervous when I start cutting." There is no need to declare that you *are* an expert, but you want to avoid admitting that you are *not* one.

Self-effacing humor is poking fun at yourself and your abilities to show that you don't take yourself too seriously. When used skillfully, it can make you appear warm, confident, and accessible. For example, when you stumble or mispronounce a word or phrase, try saying, "Take two—rewind," "The English version of that is . . . ," or "Check that."

When used poorly, humor can make you appear incompetent and lacking in confidence. There is a simple rule for using self-effacing humor. Only use it in areas where you have recognizable strengths. If you use it in areas of weakness or inexperience, it works the same way as apologies; it points out those weaknesses. Comedian Richard Pryor began his concerts with the words, "Wow, look at how many people are out there tonight. Gee, I hope I'm funny." That line got huge laughs because the audience knew he was a gifted comedian. He was making fun of his acknowledged strengths. If you were not adept at telling jokes and began by saying, "I'm going to open with a joke even though I don't tell them very well," you would be in big trouble.

Psychological research shows that employees rate their managers more accessible, brighter, and creative when the bosses use self-effacing rather than hostile humor. Here's an example of self-effacing humor, paraphrased from a speech given by the CEO of a pharmaceutical company. Jed led off by painting a picture of himself as a young CEO hanging out in a small office with his feet propped up on the desk, clueless as to how to make the company profitable. He credited the scientists who came to him, excited about the possibilities of drugs in the pipeline, with the firm's transformation into a major biotech player. He said that although it was his job to run the company, it was the scientists who were giving him something to run. The ability to make fun of yourself shows listeners how open and approachable you are. It lets them know they can ask questions or offer their views, because you exude confidence and will not be threatened.

Craft your opening with surgical precision. Draw in audience members with a snapshot of yourself, your perspective, and the insight that your presentation has been prepared exclusively for them. Be authentic. Frame the presentation with a strong visual image using similes, metaphors, or an anecdote. When possible, include sensory images other than the visual. Exude confidence and authority, and be congruent in your language and behavior. The strength and audience connection you receive from a successful opening will serve you for the entire presentation.

4

Finale

How to Close

There is an old saying in literature: "The conclusion is where the author got tired of thinking." The same principle applies to many spoken presentations. Since the fear of public speaking or delivering presentations is so prevalent, the conclusion often provides relief for the speaker. Think of the times you have heard someone telegraph that she is wrapping up by lowering the volume of her voice, running out of energy, or noticeably picking up the pace. Sprinting to the finish line, you can almost hear the voice in her head saying, "Let's end this misery and get off the stage!"

If doubts and anxiety have been building throughout your presentation, then your confidence level will be low. You may believe that, at this point, it is too late to reengage your client or audience. Is it any wonder so many presentations fizzle at the end? How often have you heard the endings, "Any questions?" "Thank you," or "Now I'd like to hand it over to X who will take the next section." What a lost opportunity! Psychologists know that we retain best the things we hear last. Given this principle, do you really want the final memory of your presentation to be a hesitant "Questions, anyone?"

When it is time to conclude your presentation, commit. Make it more important. *Increase* your level of certainty. Slow down your delivery. Keep your voice strong and steady. Make eye contact around the room. The delivery should sound as if you're employing an exclamation point, not a comma with an upward inflection. At a business talk many years ago, Deborah was given the signal that it was time to wrap up. She was not at her intended closing statement. However, she took a deep breath, slowed down, and with total commitment, delivered the next line of her talk: "So that is why business owners need to pay attention." No one knew that this line was meant to be her transition, not her conclusion. Because of the way she delivered it, it worked.

If you don't end with conviction, you are telegraphing your discomfort to the audience. If you enjoy speaking and are in control of—and passionate about—your topic, people generalize that you do business

---
End with conviction.

---

the same way. Conversely, if you are awkward, feel uncomfortable, or finish poorly, listeners can't help but generalize that *this* is how you would conduct business. If you follow that line of thinking, lowering the volume of your voice or showing any kind of relief that your presentation is over shows a lack of confidence. Speeding up demonstrates insecurity.

Delivering multiple endings signifies that you don't trust that one is sufficient. For example, "And that's why we had a 97 percent retention rate in 2008. Because our clients knew that we stood by them and had their backs. I want you to keep that confidence with you as you go into 2009. So when we're back here again next year, we will be stronger than ever." In this example, there are too many concepts crammed into the closing remarks. The speaker could have stopped after any of the first three sentences. But by adding each new sentence, he lost certainty and the clarity of one idea. An example from the world of cinema is *The Dark Knight*, which premiered in 2008.

Watch the final half hour and the multiple endings, which weakened the impact of the film.

When you run out of things to say and don't end with a firm conclusion, audience members are left wondering what you wanted them to take away from your presentation.

Why do so many presenters have difficulty with their closings? After years of coaching clients at Eloqui, we have observed that speakers spend a great deal of time developing a powerful opening and strong talking points, but they often ignore their closing. They believe it will take care of itself, or they are stumped on how best to end their talk. This lack of preparation inevitably leaves them and the audience feeling dissatisfied.

A compelling close is both elegant and potent. Don't be afraid to be dramatic or put a deliberate emphasis on your close. The opening of your presentation sets the tone. It determines how the audience will *view* you. But how you finish is typically how the audience will *remember* you. With that understanding, it is essential to place at least as much attention on how to close as on how to open. There is an old theater adage that if you begin and end well, your audience will forgive a weak middle.

> If you begin and end well, your audience will forgive a weak middle.

Follow-Through

In tennis, Peter tells us the most important part of any shot is the follow-through. If you hit the ball late, don't prepare properly, or watch the ball the whole time, you won't place the ball where you want. Watch tennis pros. A player may not win each point, but she always looks strong and graceful hitting the ball. She ends each stroke with a beautiful follow-through. Watch great presenters in business or politics. Their presentations are strong and graceful. They prepare, present, and close big.

FOLLOW YOUR INTENTION

The first thing to consider when determining how best to close is to ask yourself, "What is my intention?" or "What do I most want to achieve?" Next, ask yourself, "What is my role?" At a pharmaceutical company meeting, Eric, a sales vice president in one of their business units, had the intention to motivate the sales force to beat the previous year's numbers. The company was just coming off an amazing effort, where they had achieved 100 percent of their target in the hospital market.

Eric's challenge was to keep the effort going with a renewed sense of purpose, energy, and motivation. That is difficult once you've already won your race. So he identified individuals in the audience, acknowledged their efforts, and gave specifics of how they had conducted educational programs in the field. He praised these individuals for calling on physicians with a partner and effectively distributing medical journal reprints to educate health-care providers on what set their firm apart.

But as a good motivator (his role), Eric was also blunt about the effort it would take to overcome the inevitable inertia. He gave the sales force tangible ways to fight complacency and accomplish their new goals. He closed with his belief in their ability to push through the target goal and come back the following year having achieved even greater numbers.

CLOSING TECHNIQUES

There are a number of effective ways to close. The seven described here will guide you to fulfill your intention and bring your presentation to a successful conclusion. Your close should match your intention—simple, active, and clear. With rare exception, pick only one and do it well. Combining two or more can easily diminish the impact of your close. Conclude with a palpable sense of urgency, excitement, and commitment. Many people have a tendency to ramble or simply stop when they have delivered all their information. Your entire presentation should point toward your closing. If you want your audience to feel something, think something, or, more importantly, do something, make sure your entire presentation leads up to that.

Giving a Call to Action

When you feel extremely confident or believe the best way to move your listeners is to give them strong direction, enlist a call to action. This closing device works especially well when your objective is to motivate your audience to do something specific.

By delivering a call to action when pitching new business, you instruct your potential client to move ahead without directly asking him to hire you. One of our insurance clients, Veronica, was competing for a new piece of business. She reviewed a restaurant owner's policies before their meeting and discovered he was underinsured. At the close of their meeting, she delivered a call to action: "No matter who you hire," she said, "I recommend you increase your coverage to this amount and add a rider for this amount. I won't take you on unless you agree to this level of coverage. I don't want my clients exposed in case of an accident or claim, and I don't want to go to court." The restaurant owner liked Veronica's nerve and asked her to take over his insurance coverage, even though it meant it a greater expense for him.

> A call to action is more persuasive than selling.

A call to action is very different than selling, which focuses on why *you* are the best or would like to handle an assignment. With selling, the emphasis is on *you*. The emphasis in a call to action is on *the client* or *audience*.

Penelope is a South African physician and hospital administrator who speaks to medical professionals on the subject of burnout. After detailing the physical and mental destruction of the condition, she ends her talk with a more emotional and personal call to action:

The biggest gift you can give yourself is to remember that you are free to choose. You can choose to be a passive casualty of circumstances, blaming everyone else—just like I was. And then you get to live with frustration, helplessness, and ultimately burnout. Or you can choose to reach for the stars, develop your own personal power, and learn how to say no to being those miserable monsters, and yes to being vibrantly, joyfully alive and fulfilled.

Penelope could sharpen her call to action even more by recommending a specific task or strategy to use. The more structure and specificity you give in your call to action, the more likely your audience will follow it.

If you want to maximize the likelihood of your audience's acceptance, use the principle of minimalism. This is one of the most powerful persuasion techniques psychologists have identified and researched. The simpler the task, the more likely the audience will make the change you are recommending. Whatever you ask your listeners to do, structure it so it is as easy as possible and causes little disruption in their lives.

A well-crafted call to action also works in trainings and seminars. Tracy specializes in employee benefits, a different area of insurance from Veronica who specializes in property and casualty. Tracy conducts educational sessions in open enrollment. Once a year, she visits her manufacturing clients and, during lunch, covers changes in their medical, dental, and vision policies. At the close of a recent training, she employed the following call to action:

> Your call to action should be simple and direct.

Open the envelope from your insurance company—it's not junk mail. Make sure all the information on your new card is correct. Then shred your old ID card. Tell your pharmacist and doctor your insurance coverage has changed. Call human resources if anything is incorrect. And put your new ID card in your wallet or purse.

When delivering her call to action, note all the action verbs Tracy used—*shred* your old ID card, *open* the envelope, *tell* your pharmacist and doctor, *call* human resources, and *put* your new ID card in your wallet. Be definitive when using a call to action. It doesn't have nearly the same impact if you say, "I think it would be a good idea to maybe try and shred your old ID card." Be brief and be bold—not necessarily in that order.

> When using a call to action closing, be brief and be bold.

Bookending

Another strong method of closing is "bookending," or coming full circle and referencing your opening. Since you always know how you began your presentation, bookending is especially useful if you forget your close, never had one, or run out of time. Dave, a lawyer, was speaking to a community group on estate planning. He began his talk using his personal experience of the fires in Southern California, which ravaged hillsides and came within feet of destroying his own home. He related how, in the middle of the night, the fire department knocked on his door and told his family to evacuate. Dave had only minutes to grab a few prized possessions. He had to make major decisions under extreme pressure.

The body of his talk focused on how clients should identify what is important to them. He suggested that the audience keep records off-site and protect what is irreplaceable. After detailing the process of writing a will and establishing a trust, Dave ended with an emotional bookend. He described what it was like to smell the smoke, be nearly blinded by it, and desperately search through bedrooms to make sure his family and dog were safe and accounted for. Later, returning to find scorched hillsides but his home fortunately intact, he expressed his appreciation to the fire department and realized how this near tragedy demonstrated the importance of estate planning.

When you bookend your presentation, there is a sense of resolution and completion. The listener feels satisfied and assumes that you knew where you were going all along. Another advantage of this method is that it gives you the opportunity to add new insights in your closing that have become apparent during your talk. The idea is not to repeat exactly how you opened, but refer back to your open and add one new insight.

Bookending is one of the most frequently used devices in narrative. Movies like *American Beauty*, *The Wizard of Oz*, and *Gladiator* used this device to tease viewers with something that aroused interest but was not fully explained in the opening. The bookend neatly wrapped up each film and satisfied or resolved the initial audience interest.

> Bookending provides a sense of resolution and completion.

Recapping

The value of summarizing discussion points made in a meeting or brought to light in a more formal presentation cannot be overstated. As a speaker, you have researched your subject and spent the time and energy preparing what you want to say. When you deliver your content, you believe you have been clear and thorough. Perhaps you even observed the audience or potential client nodding in approval or smiling in agreement when you made eye contact.

However, experience tells us that throughout your presentation, the audience is sometimes distracted or not as focused as you would like. Recapping is an effective way to take charge and redirect listeners' focus. A successful close recaps those elements that drive your intention. At Eloqui, our recommendation is to recap the central three elements or key ideas. More than three are difficult for your audience or client to retain.

Here is the trick with a recap. Don't telegraph the technique by saying, "To recap," or "In summary." Starting your close this way tells audience members to stop paying attention, because they've already heard it. Instead, launch bravely into a summary of your main points. Listeners will appreciate hearing what you believe is most important for them to take away.

In a client interaction, your recap demonstrates that you have listened and can effectively highlight the company's needs and future actions. The key to active listening is to incorporate what you hear back into the conversation. When you deliver these relevant details back to the client, she feels heard and understood.

At the close of a pitch meeting to an investment banking firm, Eloqui delivered this recap: "In today's M&A market, we're impressed that you've reached the financial break-even point in only three years. Now that you're in expansion mode, we appreciate that you want your partners and associates trained in business development. But we understand you would like to wait until one of your partners returns from maternity leave in May to include her in the program. Would you like us to contact you in April to schedule the training?"

> Recap the central three points of your presentation.

With a recap, be economical and concise. You can refer to your notes or use your memory. Whenever possible, build momentum with your three primary items.

Giving an Inspirational Quote

To pique the imagination of your listener, end with an inspirational quote. At first blush, this device appears dramatic and could be perceived as over the top. However, you will be surprised at how effective a quote is when you link the words of someone well known to your message.

Chris, an insurance broker used the only quote he knew in a recent pitch to sell property and casualty insurance to an aircraft manufacturer:

> Perception and reality make strange bedfellows. Mark Twain once said, "The coldest winter I ever spent was a summer in San Francisco." On the West coast in August, you'd think it would be warm. But San Francisco summers are the coldest months of the year. In the same way, you wouldn't expect our company, Bedford, to give personalized service, considering we're the third-largest insurance firm in the country. You might think you're going to be just another account. But our clients count on us to be there, just like San Francisco expects the fog to roll in all summer. Our 98.5 percent client retention backs that up.

Another client of ours, Woody, gave a talk to business professionals about how to take the time to appreciate those closest to them, both in business and their personal lives. To make his point, he described his time with his own father and ended with an inspirational quote.

> I knew I had done everything possible to make my father's last days peaceful, loving, and serene. I fulfilled my purpose and achieved inner peace as I had not experienced before. And I felt this calm come over me like a warm, cozy blanket. As Carl Jung wrote many years ago, "As far as we can discern, the sole purpose of human existence is to kindle a light in the darkness of mere being."

A leader in the Democratic Party had been taken to task for not being more vocal about criticizing the Bush administration for the war in Iraq, the economic meltdown, or the response to Hurricane Katrina. In response, He Who Shall Remain Nameless used one of our favorite quotes from Napoleon in the closing of his presentation on the track record of the Bush administration: "Never interrupt your enemy when he's making a mistake."

When constructing a presentation, you can find a plethora of quotes at http://quotationspage.com, http://wisdomquotes.com, or http://brainyquotes.com. You can also visit any library or used-book store for the weighty volumes that contain various forms of quotes. When using the Internet, think about a word that describes your message and type it in to see who has used it in a speech or conversation. For example, if you want to motivate your team, look up *success, vision, challenges*, or *victory* to find appropriate quotes.

Inspirational quotes can be both dramatic and persuasive.

Here's a good rule of thumb with quotes. Reference someone who is long dead or not terribly famous so that your audience doesn't have an opinion about his or her politics or lifestyle, which could adversely color your message. Or attribute a quote to a family member—either real or imagined. Simply lead off with "As my Aunt Tilly used to say, . . ."

Surprise

To vary the construction of a quote, add the name of the author at the end. During a political race, candidates frequently enlist this technique. They deliver a powerful quote that we believe is from a member of their party, yet when they mention the author, it is someone from the opposing party. This element of surprise grabs our attention. The essential ingredient is discovering the name of the person and realizing it was not who you expected.

Using Triplicates

From orators in the Roman Senate to southern preachers and politicians, speakers for centuries have invoked the power of repetition for a dramatic finish—using the same word or phrase multiple times to initiate closing statements. These phrases include "I believe," "We will," "I know," or "We envision." Triplicate is an Eloqui technique that takes the ancient Greek rhetorical concept of Anaphora (the repetition of a word or phrase at the beginning of successive phrases, clauses, or lines) but refines it with a twist, using only three as a means of sounding more resolute and certain. The use of triplicate evokes an emotional response. This is, in large part, because of the repetition and the metered language, which suggests an incantation. According to the *American Heritage Dictionary*, "An incantation is a recitation of verbal charms or spells to produce a magical effect." We believe speakers can apply triplicate words, phrases, or sounds in the same magical way.

When employing triplicates, save the best for last. Build the importance of your three statements, so that the third is the payoff. The same is true of your delivery. Build the emphasis according to the ascending power of the content. An Eloqui example of a triplicate might sound like this:

> *We believe* anyone can learn to speak in their unique voice . . . *We believe* when people speak authentically, they are more persuasive. . . . And *we believe* if authenticity were the standard of communication, business dialogue would be forever transformed.

An alternative way to use the triplicate form is to tell a short story. For example:

> I know skiing down this double black diamond run seems like suicide. But I also know if I traverse the slope and control my speed, I just may get to the bottom in one piece. And I know at

the end of the run, I will have the courage to attempt other challenges without fear.

Note the more intellectual, rather than emotional, focus in the following example:

I can see how your "best in class" focus has been the key to your success. I can see that your company will continue to grow exponentially in the coming years. And I can see why it is vital that you partner with a fellow "best in class" company to support that growth.

An alternative way to craft a message with the triplicate format is to use phrases or words that are associated but not identical, as in the following:

We *appreciate* the difficulty of competing for new business when you have been trained as an accountant. We *understand* that developing elevator speeches is difficult, even though it will encourage more networking. But we *know* that business will come to you as a result of differentiating your services.

George, the CEO of a major charitable foundation, was speaking to the board of directors at the annual meeting. After acknowledging their accomplishments, George wanted to motivate the contributors and volunteers to achieve even more going forward:

It is the power of you that created this great organization to improve lives and find a cure. It is the power of you that produced the success of this year. And it is the power of you that will take us to new heights of improving the lives of the people we serve and finding a cure.

It is possible to nullify the impact of the triplicate technique by being too dramatic. To maintain the integrity of triplicates, under play the delivery but keep the commitment. Using a triplicate is a great way to build the power of your message. It is very important to understand *when* to use this method. The triplicate signals the end of your presentation. If you continue speaking after that, it will sound odd or you will be stepping on your applause.

> When using triplicates in your closing, save the strongest point for last.

Revisiting Your Theme

In music, a theme is one of the major melodies of a piece. It creates an emotional effect by being familiar, even though it may be played by different instruments or at different tempos. And hearing a familiar theme allows the listener to reconnect with "home base."

In speaking, we define a theme as an easily repeatable phrase, such as the following:

- ▪ "We try harder."
- ▪ "It's the right thing to do."
- ▪ "Who holds the power in your business?"

Themes in presentations are similar to slogans in that they ground the concept and enhance the meaning of your content. Think of them as the core or central idea. Often times, your open will suggest a theme. Ending your talk by revisiting your theme says, "This is what I want you to remember."

Because themes are short and catchy, they tend to be memorable. Used sparingly throughout your presentation, they stitch together the content. This is different from the old speaker axiom "Tell 'em what you're going to tell 'em, tell 'em what you told 'em, and tell 'em again," which we find patronizing and clunky. Each time you revisit a theme, repeat it exactly, deliver it with a variation, or add something new to pique the listener's imagination. Whenever possible, expand on the meaning instead of hammering a point home with simple repetition.

When you close with your theme, the audience feels satisfied. You have achieved resolution. One of our marketing clients, Sheri, gave a talk titled Your Brand Is Your Promise to a business group. The presentation was about how to attract new business through strategic marketing. Her theme was that everything supports your promise. Notice how Sheri incorporated her theme multiple times in a client pitch:

> When you reference your theme, feel free to expand on its meaning.

I have clients in property management whose new business had stalled. They forgot that everything supports their promise. They weren't doing any marketing and realized they never would unless they had help.

So we came in and updated their look, working with a designer who used the same colors of red and grey to maintain continuity, and gave their collateral material a more contemporary look by changing the font and wording to make it proactive and strong. Everything supported their promise.

We implemented a direct-mail campaign, placed articles in the trades in front of their target markets, and increased their visibility. We included quotes from clients that emphasized "The way they manage buildings maximizes the value." Now that's what we say in all their materials, because everything supports their promise.

Themes are often used to inspire or motivate. They need to be strong and emphasized when delivered rather than buried in the text. There is strength to themes that you want to convey to your audience.

> Don't bury your theme.

In Chapter 3, we used the example of Mark, a congregation president's Yom Kippur speech to highlight the use of themes. Note how the end of his talk folded in his theme that gifts come in unexpected packages:

Yes, we are all given God's gifts, and yes, sometimes gifts arrive in unexpected packages. My gift arrived in the form of a child with many special needs. Your gift may have arrived in another unexpected package. The important thing is how we deal with them.

Yom Kippur is the day we stand before God and ask to be inscribed in the book of life for the coming year. It is a perfect time for each of us to look around at the gifts we have been given and ask, "What have I done with these gifts?" Today, on Yom Kippur, I ask you to take these gifts and use them as a contribution to our community, our congregation, and the world.

Telling a Personal Anecdote or Case Study

At times the most powerfully persuasive ending is one that comes from your own experience. Telling a personal anecdote demonstrates your investment, your understanding, and your empathy.

> Telling a personal anecdote in your closing demonstrates your investment, your understanding, and your empathy.

Danielle, a successful shoe designer was auditioning at a cable channel to host a new reality TV show on home decorating. She ended the audition with her own experience:

I'd been remodeling our home in Manhattan Beach, when I found a tear sheet from a decorating magazine of a great pocket door. This one had see-through glass instead of the standard wood frame. I loved it, so I had it custom built in red! Unfortunately, after picking out the tile and granite, the molding and stainless steel sink, I realized that all you noticed was the red door which overshadowed everything else. As a designer, I know better and strive to have all the elements in balance. It was a big mistake. And sometimes that happens. So I appreciate what the participants go through, especially with limited budgets and time!

Sonja focuses on health-care insurance for midsized firms. A new offering from one of her carriers is a mobile screening unit that travels to individual businesses. She has no trouble stressing the importance of using this unit when she references her own experience:

I just returned from Minnesota, where we buried my kid sister. She was the health nut in the family, so no one ever thought about her getting sick. Laurie had her twenty-year high school reunion coming up, so she went on a weight-loss program. As the weight came off, she noticed a lump in her breast. By the time they diagnosed it in the lab, the cancer had spread throughout her body. The ironic thing is that her company had a mobile screening unit that came on-site every three months. If my sister had taken just a half hour out of her workday to have a mammogram, she might still be alive today.

The other advantage of telling a story at the close is that it links together the key elements of your presentation. Narrative is the best way to explain general concepts and make them specific. We only remember details when they are grounded or embedded in associative images. So in the example of Sonja's sister, we're linking good health with a mobile screening unit parked right outside her office. In Danielle's case, making the mistake of choosing the red door allowed her to better understand and empathize with what nonprofessional designers appearing on the show would go through.

Identifying with the participants in a story is much easier than intellectualizing. When we were kids, our mothers told us repeatedly how good spinach was for us, but only when we watched Popeye down a can and instantly grow muscles to rescue Olive Oyl did we mimic his behavior. Life isn't that different for adults. There are so many things on our plates, it's easy to put off what we know is good for us. At a recent family law seminar, Archie, an attorney, ended with this story:

> My client Bill was going through an acrimonious divorce. He and his wife fought constantly, but the saving grace for Bill was that soon it would be over and he could move on with his life. I encouraged him to change the beneficiaries on all his insurance policies, but he never got around to it. What none of us realized was the level of stress Bill was under. He unexpectedly had a heart attack and died. Counter to his intent, his ex-wife received all of his assets. Because Bill hadn't changed the documents, we couldn't fight the legal system.

When you end with a personal story, you lock the message into your listener's long-term memory. Be clear and strong in both the open *and* close of any presentation.

CLOSE THE DEAL

Typically, our clients finish their pitch by asking for the business. Even though getting the business is their intention, asking for it can come across as desperate, awkward, or off-putting to the potential client. Resist the urge to ask for the deal, say you're the best, or tell how you look forward to working together. These phrases may sound forthright, but they come from a weak position and actually reduce your odds of success—doing so puts the focus on you as the seller and not on your audience, your potential clients. Many cli-

> Closing a presentation by asking for a deal is ineffective and reduces your chances for success.

ents report that such a direct appeal makes them feel pressured and uncomfortable.

Instead, you can always say what you're passionate about or how you've solved similar problems for other clients. For example, when Eloqui is trying to land a new client, we might say, "The closer to the actual pitch and the higher the stakes, the more we enjoy coming in and applying our team presenting skills so our clients win."

People like to make up their own minds in deciding whether or not to hire you. You should rarely have to ask for the business unless a potential client has been on the fence for a long time or you have expended the limit of your patience and you're ready to walk away. For most business interactions, if you have properly identified a client's needs and established your credibility, he or she will ask *you* how to proceed.

Knowing all this, it is still difficult to depart from the traditional way of closing. The next time you are in a client pitch with a lot riding on the outcome, tell an appropriate anecdote. Use information you have culled from researching the firm and listening to the client to make assumptions about its needs. Weave that information into a relevant story of how you assisted another client with a similar problem. Make the listener see herself and identify with the scenario. Trust that she will be convinced to enlist your services without doing a commercial at the end of your presentation.

Eloqui is frequently asked how to end an elevator speech, especially if it features only one aspect of the business or services. Delivering an overview of all your services dilutes your message. It can't help but sound general and is not memorable. Since we recommend describing only *one* aspect per elevator speech, the question is how do you let people know about all the other services your firm offers?

The answer is a tagline. This conclusion is a catch-bin phrase that briefly includes what else you do. For example, if we had focused our Eloqui elevator speech on working with pitch teams, our tagline might have been "In addition to winning your next beauty contest, Eloqui trains sales teams to differentiate their services, delivers keynotes at conferences, and coaches individuals for upcoming speeches. I'm Jeannie Alan of Eloqui." Or you can end with your slogan, such as "We are the counsel you keep," "We bring cash from chaos," or "Unlock the power of your team."

A CLOSE TO THE CHAPTER ON CLOSING

In Bill Clinton's book, *My Life: The Presidential Years*, he reprints a speech he gave at a Masonic temple, the place of worship where Martin Luther King, Jr., gave his last speech. Note the variety of techniques Clinton uses for both the opening and closing (including bookends, triplicate, and an implied call to action). In business presentations, we recommend clarity and economy in choosing and delivering a close. In a house of workshop or a non-business setting, audiences will respond to a more theatrical and inspirational approach. In your opinion, when reading the following text, are there too many techniques or, in this particular venue, the right amount?

Open

If Martin Luther King were to reappear by my side today and give us a report card on the last twenty-five years, what would he say? You did a good job, he would say, voting and electing people who formerly were not electable because of the color of their skin. . . . You did a good job, he would say, letting people who have the ability to do so live wherever they want to live, go wherever they want to go in this great country. . . . He would say you did a good job creating a black middle class . . . in opening opportunity.

Close

So in this pulpit, on this day, let me ask all of you in your heart to say: We will honor the life and the work of Martin Luther King. . . . Somehow, by God's grace, we will turn this around. We will give these children a future. We will take away their guns and give them books. We will take away their despair and give them hope. We will rebuild the families and the neighborhoods and the communities. We won't make all the work that has gone on here benefit just a few. We will do it together, by the grace of God.

In the same way, we hope you have given up the despair of not being able to close your presentation and are now armed with practical tools. Your closing is the bridge to a bright future with your audience or client.

5

For Example

The Power of Narrative

The roar was deafening. My stomach was in knots. Because I was the lightest, I was at the back of the plane. On my bottom, I inched slowly forward, dreading what was to come. There was no turning back now, unless I lost my nerve and rode the plane back to the airstrip. Glancing out the window, my fellow travelers were colorful specks, drifting on currents of air. Suddenly it was my turn. When I was on my feet and gripping the struts, the flight instructor put her hand against my back and gave a gentle push. With the biggest leap of faith I have ever taken, I dove out the cavernous opening, arms spread like wings and feet extended behind me. My mouth opened to scream, but nothing came out. Somehow I managed to pull the rip cord and felt the parachute open. I will never forget the brilliant blue, red, and yellow billowing canopy above me. At that moment, it was the most beautiful thing I'd ever seen in my life. The joy was indescribable.

This is the story I told to open my talk to women executives of the National Association of Women Business Owners (NAWBO). My topic was on women finding their voice. To grab the attention of the audience right away and establish a connection, I delivered a story from my own experience. I also felt pressure to be compelling. Since the audience considered me a communication specialist, I worried that a case of nerves might affect my delivery. But by using a story where anxiety was already in play, no one would be the wiser; my anxiety would actually help me tell it more effectively.

The analogy of skydiving to the fear of public speaking had potential but needed a clear, strong link. Without the link, or comparison between the two activities, the impact would be lost. This is how I joined the two:

> Jumping out of a plane is similar to what many of our clients feel when giving a speech. "It seemed like a good idea at the time, but what was I thinking?" Emotions run the gamut from exhilaration to sheer panic. Anxiety sets in like an unwelcome visitor. Time becomes elastic. There is a sense you're on a speeding train that takes forever to arrive at the station. Right before your presentation, your entire surroundings are in supersharp focus. Your breathing is shallow or irregular. Some recall an out-of-body experience. Yet somehow you dive off the cliff and begin. And then it's over. You made it through in one piece. In fact, people were moved. You were successful and accomplished your goal.

For a week after jumping out of the plane and landing safely on the ground, I felt invincible. I basked in my success. Performers will tell you that when they connect with their audience, there is no better feeling. There are risks to making public presentations, but there are also huge rewards. And once you commit to speaking, there are tools and techniques to find your own voice.

EDUCATE = THINK VERSUS PERSUADE = ACT

People respond to stories more than a well-constructed collection of facts and statistics. Hearing an engaging story makes the listener want to know what comes next and gets him or her firmly on your side. A good story sets the stage, creates a visual frame, and becomes the jumping-off point for greater understanding. Whether in business or at a charitable or social function, stories are the cultural glue that binds us together, eliciting empathy, compassion, and buy-in.

> A good story sets the stage, creates a visual frame, and is a speaker's most persuasive tool.

In business, stories are valuable tools for engineering the perception you wish to create. For example, when Eloqui was newly formed, we were considered "speaker coaches" who would be called on prior to sales meetings or product launches to work with an executive on his or her keynote speech. In truth, training and coaching in this capacity was only about 20 percent of our business. Our bread and butter is training small groups within companies to become successful pitch teams, to use effective networking strategies in the business community, and to develop leadership skills.

To change the perception that we were primarily speaker coaches, David and I had to tell stories that contained a different message. Instead of focusing on individuals who were successful or experienced less anxiety after taking our course, we needed to emphasize the benefits for teams. Companies are always looking for ways to drive business and measure their return on investment, especially during tough economic times. Eloqui stories had to include the specifics of how our clients became more successful and profitable because of their new communication skills. Quantifiable results that increased sales turned the perception of the skills we taught from "soft" to "hard." A story directed toward this purpose is based on MPM, an advertising agency in Glendale, California:

One week after they contacted Eloqui, MPM was pitching a large insurance company in Portland that wanted to expand its footprint in the Latino community. The agency that won the pitch would create sizable inroads for their client in this profitable marketplace. Anxiety was high because so much was at stake. Added to that, the CEO of MPM had assigned his Latino ad execs to drive the entire presentation, but this team had never carried a complete pitch before.

There was no time in their schedule to work with Eloqui until the day before the pitch. David and I arrived to see a final run-through and ostensibly to give a few notes before signing off on their presentation. At this late date, no one wanted to change what they had prepared. We knew whatever we said would be weighed against the ticking clock. During the rehearsal, the ad execs began by introducing themselves and relating their backgrounds, which the insurance client had asked them to do. Yet talking about themselves made each of them uncomfortable. They were also missing the point. We knew that even though the insurance company had requested self-introductions, the typical client only cares about its own needs and what the vendor can do for them.

We probed for what else they had. They showed us a video of their successes, which they were planning to include later in the pitch; it was perfect. We recommended that MPM do the unexpected, lead off with the video and then link their introductions to what they do for their clients, as demonstrated in the video.

Then we assigned Miriam, a charming, articulate member of the team, the role of facilitator. We directed her to say why each person on the team was present at the meeting, based on what they would do for the client once MPM was awarded the contract. We coached Miriam on how to keep the agenda on track and support the members who might struggle.

We listened and reshaped the anecdotes of all the team members, so they sounded authentic and engaging. We practiced hand-offs until they were seamless. And we encouraged them to exhibit their enthusiasm, which ultimately reduced their anxiety.

MPM not only won the pitch and brought a new client on board, but team members now knew they could count on each other to serve as a pitch team and go after more business in the Latino market.

Although this story focuses on the success of MPM, it highlights the specifics of what Eloqui does when called on to work within companies. Yet if we were to say merely that we encourage our clients and give them practical skills, it would be much less effective than to wrap those elements into a story like this one. The goal is to engage the listener, who draws his or her own conclusions.

FOLLOW THE MONEY

Another client of ours, Gary, decided to leave a major financial firm and begin his own consulting practice. We interviewed him to find out what kind of clients he believed were necessary to grow his fledgling business. We encouraged him to look back through his experience and recall the success stories of particular clients who fit this profile. To grow his practice, these were the individuals Gary needed to feature in his anecdotes when pitching potential clients and networking. One of our advisors calls it "following the money."

Gary's prime targets were married professionals. He crafted the following story to appeal to other couples who were busy juggling family and business lives:

> It took one month to set up the first meeting with Alex and Jamie. Between working fifty hours a week, dragging their kids to after-school activities, and trying to squeeze in a dinner date with each other, they were exhausted. Their finances were a mess, and they felt like their spending was out of control. Added to that, Jamie wanted to leave her company and start her own business, but she had no idea how to plan for it financially.

I shared that I understood, having two kids of my own. I interviewed them at length and determined they were more conservative than they realized. Then I analyzed their spending and cash flow and created a working budget. I reconstructed their portfolio, while also minimizing taxes. I reviewed their college plan for their first child and learned that Alex had chosen a savings plan for a teenager about to start college rather than for their toddler. This meant they could choose a less aggressive option. After I crafted a household budget, Alex and Jamie were also able to save money every month for their second child's college education.

Now that we are working together, Alex and Jamie have a clearer vision of where they will be financially in the next five years. They have a better understanding of what types of investments they own and what purposes each serves.

Jamie decided to leave the big firm and go out on her own. Now her career is more fulfilling. And surprisingly, they were able to take their first real vacation to Hawaii, which cost them ten thousand dollars but was planned for and well within their budget.

When potential clients and colleagues listen to this story, they have a tangible sense of Gary's commitment, creative thinking, and long-term associations with his clients. But if he were to state these attributes, they would be much less believable. In listing his accomplishments, he would also run the risk of sounding arrogant. This is not a concern with a well-told story.

> A well-told story highlights your achievements and conveys your skills without the need to brag.

ESSENTIAL ELEMENTS

By telling an anecdote, you demonstrate your personal investment by revealing what is important to you from your direct experience, your upbringing, or learning from your mistakes. The weaker position, and one we hear in so many presentations, is a statement like "This is important," or "You need to do this." People don't like being told what they should or shouldn't do. However, a well-crafted anecdote makes the point without any qualifiers, apologies, or arrogance.

Ben, a labor attorney from Ventura County, is an effective speaker lecturing on what companies need to do to avoid legal hassles with their employees. He typically begins his presentations with a comment that tells his audience that if they listen to him, he will keep them out of jail. This is compelling but doesn't reveal his personal investment, except from a legal perspective. In our first session with Ben, we discovered he had an insider's understanding of what his clients were facing. Here is one of the stories that he now tells to lead off his training on employee rules and regulations:

> A well-crafted anecdote can make your point without qualifiers, apologies, or arrogance.

For her summer job, my seventeen-year-old daughter, Jill, came to work for our law firm. She was assigned administrative tasks in what we call "the dungeon." It's the basement where client folders are organized, indexed, and filed. After she'd been working a couple of days, I asked Jill how it was going. She said, "Dad, it's brutal. I've got paper cuts. I'm balancing on chairs. I've had to change my clothes because it's so dirty. And by the way, when do I take lunch? And if I take a shorter lunch, can I leave early?" While Jill was talking, I was thinking to myself, "Oh, no. Workers' comp, OSHA, overtime penalties, meals, and rest breaks." My own firm had failed to advise a part-time worker of her schedule and rights. It made me realize how easy it is to overlook what we are required by law to cover with our workers.

What if your listener doesn't understand what it is you do, even though you think you're being clear? Frame your services in an anec-

Link your story to something
your audience understands
or needs from you.

dote, and whenever possible, link them to something he or she does understand. In the following example, Phil, the vice president of insurance services tied to a major bank, told a story linked to a well-known Las Vegas hotel:

I was standing in my living room drinking a cup of coffee, watching the news, when an announcer said, "Last night the Sands Hotel was blown up in a spectacular display of pyrotechnics to make way for the building of the Venetian." I was stunned, because I was the broker on that placement. And there was no coverage. That meant if there was a loss, my client was totally exposed! And not only would he be liable for damages, but worse, he potentially could not build the Venetian.

Now understand that we had gone to London to place their implosion coverage. We'd negotiated the price. We'd received approval from the underwriters. It was all lined up. And the only caveat was that the London underwriter wanted twenty-four hours' notice *before* the explosion so he could initiate coverage. But the consultant on the account had failed to call us in advance, so the building was blown up *without* coverage.

We rallied all of our team members. I immediately called the underwriter in London, found out our potential liabilities, and asked that he backdate coverage by twenty-four hours. I convinced him that the building was blown up in the middle of the night. No one was on the street. It was not done for a media event. And we were in line with his original intent. He said he would get back to us.

For me, the next couple of hours were agonizing. Finally, the underwriter called back and agreed to backdate the policy if the duration of coverage was shortened for any losses that might come in after the fact. I called my client with the news, and he agreed before I even finished my statement.

So not only did my client receive the original coverage, but two months later, when someone came forward and said he was hit on the head with a rock, which could not have come from any other place except the street surrounding the Sands, my client was covered. And the building of the Venetian proceeded on schedule.

When you incorporate specific details, the listener will relate to your story even if he or she hasn't had the same experience or isn't directly connected to the anecdote you are telling. The more specific the story, the better. Did you picture the Sands being blown up when you read this story? Did you picture Phil standing in front of the TV, holding a cup of coffee? In your imagination, was he wearing a robe or business suit? To ensure listeners play the movie in their heads, you need to provide specifics. Although it takes only a few details to provide the basis for visualization, it's impossible to picture generalities. For example, "We helped a client solve their toughest problem," is too general and cannot be visualized. We're taught to be general to be inclusive. In reality, the opposite is true. You gain traction and your message sticks when you are concrete enough to make the audience "see" your story.

> The more specific the story, the better. Polite generalities miss the mark.

CUSTOMIZATION

To be most effective, base your anecdote on the audience's experience or area of interest. If you are pitching to lawyers, they want to know what success you've had with other law firms. The same applies to accounting, insurance, and financial services.

Our client Charlotte, who is with a well-known private wealth management firm, could only tell the following anecdote to CPAs, CFOs, or a company CEO. It is too technical for a general audience.

However, the technical aspects are exactly why it is compelling to financial types:

> We have a client in Valencia who is a landscape contractor. Mature company, healthy cash flow. But their taxes were high, so they were looking for ways to move their money outside their corporation and relieve their tax burden. We analyzed and broke down their situation. We looked at the entities they had and their overall objective. We recommended a captive insurance company and partnered with their attorney and CPA, while managing the money inside that structure. This allowed the client to defer $1.2 million in taxes, get the write-off as a business deduction, and change the character of that income from ordinary to capital gains. So they ended up enjoying not only tax relief, but also asset protection, building control claims, and estate-planning benefits.

When listeners can identify, understand, and put themselves into the scenario, they are engaged. Their experience may vary somewhat, but if the core elements of a story are applicable, it is enough to draw them in. And perhaps the best quality of a well-told story or client anecdote is that it becomes portable—listeners will retell it to others.

The most memorable presentations include stories whenever possible. The next section will give you tools to organize your material into persuasive anecdotes, using techniques from our work with professionals, concepts from our fellow advisors, and theatrical templates from the world of improvisation.

> Tailor your story to your audience.

BUSINESS ANECDOTES

When David and I began attending networking functions, we would frequently hear professionals tell client anecdotes describing their product or services. A large percentage of these anecdotes were ineffective, boring, rambling, and off-point. Typically, they contained too much context (or background) and often diminished, or left out entirely, what the professional did to serve his or her clients.

Part of the problem is what the Heath brothers, in their book *Made to Stick*, have called the "curse of knowledge." When professionals use abbreviations and acronyms or leave out specifics entirely, it is because they are removed from the original state of not-knowing and have forgotten who their audience is. They make an incorrect assumption that their audience knows what *they* know. By failing to provide specifics, concrete language, or insights into how they operate, they fail to convince the audience why they should be hired or referred to other clients.

The next time you make a presentation, remember that only *you* hear the melody; the audience only hears the tapping. This means that you have to tap in a way that makes the song clear. This is

Happy Birthday to You

Elizabeth Newton earned a Ph.D. in psychology at Stanford University for the following study regarding the curse of knowledge. Her study shows the difference between what a presenter *thinks* she is saying and what the audience gets from it.

In this experiment, there were two groups: tappers and listeners. The tappers were directed to tap out the rhythm of a common song ("Happy Birthday"), and the listeners were asked to identify it. The tappers predicted that the listeners would correctly identify the song more than 80 percent of the time. The results showed that it was less than 15 percent. Why was there such a huge discrepancy? The tappers admitted that as they were tapping, they were also singing the melody to themselves, but the listeners only heard the tapping; they didn't have the knowledge the tappers were sure they had.

why anecdotes convey meaning much better than data and bullet points.

The OSB Template

Effective anecdotes are not difficult to construct. First, determine what kind of business you would like more of. This is what Eloqui did when shifting its image from speaker coaches to team trainers or what Gary did when approaching young couples to grow his business. Consider the impression you would like to create or the one message you would like to deliver, then pick the client anecdote that best delivers this impression. Your entire professional career and personal experience contains stories that can be shaped according to the objective or impression you would like to achieve.

> When crafting stories, determine the one impression or message that is most important and choose the anecdote that best delivers it.

Apply the Eloqui template of obstacle, solution, and benefit (OSB). This three-act mini-play includes only the essential elements of business storytelling. The idea is to tell a compelling anecdote in thirty seconds to two minutes—the amount of time you can effectively hold an audience's interest in a networking meeting or in response to the question "What is it you do?"

> Remember OSB (obstacle, solution, and benefit).

Obstacle. The first act is the obstacle, or challenge that the client was facing. Interestingly enough, people need very little context or background to become engaged in your story. Listen to great storytellers. Look back at your favorite books, movies, or plays. Most begin with a dramatic challenge or obstacle, providing just enough context to draw you in. Perhaps the most notorious opening line of a book is "It was a dark and stormy night." As a dramatic hook, use the same technique when beginning your anecdote.

One Eloqui OSB begins with "A custom publishing company in Atlanta found out its largest client of the last ten years was putting their contract out to bid." Do you want to hear more? Can you relate or empathize? Do you have to be in publishing to understand the problem?

As long as the audience can visualize the "players" and relate to their challenges, you keep your listeners' attention. (Note: to aid in visualization, be sure to add a descriptive adjective to the characters in your story, and assign a name to key players to keep them distinct.) If you don't start with a strong obstacle, their minds wander, and it is extremely difficult to draw them back in. Consider the traditional ways professionals tee up their anecdotes, such as "Let me tell you a funny story"; "We solved a problem for a client and saved the company millions of dollars. This is how we did it"; or "A custom publishing company in Atlanta was founded in 1965 and had sixteen divisions specializing in everything from magazine production to Internet surveys." These outmoded forms of construction cause you to lose traction right from the beginning.

> An effective story starts with an obstacle.

To make the obstacle more compelling, include what was at stake and how it was time sensitive. In the case of the publishing company, we would add "This contract was worth $5 million per year, and if lost, the firm would likely go under. Also, the pitch was in two weeks, and the publishing company was up against two larger and more well-connected firms from Chicago and New York." The goal is to have listeners say to themselves, "What happened next?" (For a complete description of this anecdote, see the story of On Point in Chapter 2.)

Solution. Once you have related the obstacle, move on to the solution act of the play. Be careful not to begin the solution and then go back to describe more obstacles. Pacing, momentum,

> The "Solution" is where you get to demonstrate what sets you apart.

and clarity are all key elements of a good story, so keep moving forward. In the solution is where you get to relate all the compelling services you deliver to your clients. This act is the appropriate place for saying what you do differently than other service providers without reading your résumé. Told correctly, we see you *exhibiting* these traits rather than reciting a list of services you provide.

It is important to use concrete language when describing your solution. These precise terms will set you apart. Envision a mechanic about to work on your car. He lifts the hood, assesses the problem, and then picks up the right tool (such as a socket wrench or a screwdriver). Consider what mechanical terms best describe your actions. Did you analyze, craft, design, implement, or persuade? These active verbs allow the listener to envision and reenact your efforts. We literally see how you operate. (In the appendix, we've included a list of active verbs to trigger your imagination.)

> Use concrete terms so the listener can visualize what you do.

When describing the solution, our clients frequently say they "worked with" or "helped" their clients. Such terms are endemic throughout business vocabulary, but they are not specific. The audience doesn't see your value or appreciate what you did that was special. Diminishing your role will result in being commoditized; your value will be unclear and contracting for your services will be based on price.

> Choose specific, action-oriented verbs for your stories.

Perhaps you have been in business for a long time, and what you do seems simple or straightforward. It may be for you, but that's not the message you want to deliver to your audience or client. Besides, your success is based on years of experience, know-how, and nurtured contacts. Consider what Phil, the VP at the insurance firm achieved with the London underwriter, persuading him to backdate

---

The Triad

Construct a list of three specific actions using active verbs. People tend to respond to units of three. Consider classic children's stories and nursery rhymes involving trios—the Three Little Pigs, Goldilocks and the Three Bears, and Three Blind Mice. Modern plays are always three acts. Going back to ancient Rome, one of Cicero's favorite techniques to emphasize key points was called a tricolon, which is a series of three parallel words, phrases, or clauses. The most familiar example is Julius Caesar's "Veni, vidi, vici," or "I came, I saw, I conquered." Even Aristotle said a story must have a beginning, a middle, and an end. He prescribed three elements for any good speech: logos, pathos, and ethos (that is, thought, emotion, and the character of the speaker).

---

coverage by twenty-four hours to cover the implosion of the Vegas hotel. Only someone with Phil's experience could have negotiated that transaction.

We have been asked by our clients whether to use *we* or *I* statements in describing their solution. It depends on the circumstances. Do you want to promote your team? If so, use *we*. Are you new to the job and short on anecdotes? Interview your team members and tell *their* stories—using *we*. However, if you are promoting your individual efforts as a trusted advisor or sole practitioner, it may be more appropriate to use an *I* statement. You do not have to sound self-promoting. When you describe the solution, inject your enthusiasm, passion, and caring for the client. Listeners will arrive at the correct conclusion.

To make your solution more compelling, add phrases like "what my client didn't expect," "what we discovered," or "what was revealed." This element of surprise draws listeners in and makes them pay closer attention. Whenever you share an unexpected or surprising discovery, they want to know what happened. Storytellers since the beginning of time have used this element of surprise to keep audiences engaged. Even in business, you are a performer telling a story. Accept this axiom and you will be successful.

Benefit. The third act of the OSB template is the benefit. Businesspeople are especially attuned to how your actions contribute to the client's success. Most benefits are expected; for example, you won the pitch, you saved your client a certain number of dollars, or you kept the company from being sued. But for a strong and memorable close to an anecdote, also give the *unexpected* benefit. If you can't think of one, try completing the phrase "Going forward, my client now realizes . . ." If there has been a transformational experience, identify it. Or describe how the client now does business differently. With MPM, the advertising company going after the Portland client, the benefit was winning the pitch. But the unexpected benefit was the team's newfound confidence and skill to go after other, larger clients that focused on the Latino market. Examine each incident for a compelling, unanticipated outcome. This "aha" moment provides a rich opportunity for audiences and clients to see you in a special light. And as we know, great stories have great endings.

> Use the element of surprise and highlight unexpected benefits of your services.

Go back and read through the Miriam, Phil, and Gary stories in this chapter. Apply the OSB template to identify the structure, pacing, and active verbs included in each. Did they hook you? Did you visualize the process as you read them? Do you have a better understanding now of what each individual or company does that is distinct from their competitors? Finally, judge the effectiveness of these stories compared to that of other anecdotes you hear at networking meetings or business events.

Alternate Story Template

There are times when OSB will not serve your purpose. For instance, when you would like to share a story where a transformation or lessons learned are the essence of your interaction, another template may better suit your objective. Even though a story has to have a beginning, a middle, and an end, these elements do not have to be linear. You can consider story progression as circular and begin anywhere along the circumference of a circle, as long as it has a meaningful conclusion. The following alternative template is derived from the world of improvisational theater and has been adapted for business purposes; there is a brief explanation of what each line accomplishes:

1. "I have a client who . . ." or "Once I worked on a project that . . ." (identifies a character or theme)
2. "Every day (week, month, or year) . . ." (establishes a routine)
3. "Until one day . . ." (breaks the routine)
4. "Because of that, . . ." (faces the consequences)
5. "And because of that, . . ." (faces the consequences of the consequences)
6. "Until finally . . ." (brings the developments to a head)
7. "Ever since that time, . . ." (resolves the issue into a new reality)

Like when you're learning to ride a bicycle, you first need to practice with training wheels. To practice with this template, that means telling a fictional anecdote—the more outrageous, the better! In a group, have one person take each line. Because you have no idea what the person before you will say, you cannot think ahead and fill in the blank. Have fun with it and let your imagination loose. I would employ a version of this template, called the Never-ending Story, with young children. Children have an unbridled freedom to be creative. They will express their own version of the world through colorful characters and improbable transactions.

For example, a group of seven-year-old girls told a version of the following story:

> Once there was a frog who sang opera. Every day, while the rest of his family croaked to each other, Teddy practiced hitting a high C. The rest of the frogs had to cover their ears because Teddy's singing made them crazy. His mother worried that he would never amount to anything.
>
> Until one day, Teddy saw a fire coming close to the town. He hopped to the firehouse and sang his froggy heart out. Because of that, the firefighters stopped eating dinner and came out to see who was making all the racket. And because of that, Teddy sang like never before. When they tried to catch him and put him on the local news, he hopped away toward the fire, and they had to chase him.
>
> Until finally, they saw the fire, rang the bell, and took off in the fire engine. And ever since that day, the firefighters no longer need the fire bell. Teddy's singing lets them know when a fire is nearby.

Now try applying this template to a client interaction. Make each line brief and keep the story moving. The template will lead you through a logical progression. When you begin, first give the client or project a vivid descriptor or challenge. For example, "We have a CEO client in insurance who micromanages all of her top executives." (I admit, the CEO is not as colorful as Teddy the frog, but there are limits to how colorful we can be in business.)

Here are a few more examples of opening lines with vivid descriptors of potential characters to spark your imagination and jump-start the exercise:

- Linda was the most compassionate HR director we ever had, until we learned she was stealing from the company.
- Harry, the leading rainmaker of a Century City law firm, wanted to retire and still receive his seven-figure income.
- Jones never gave a talk without a boring PowerPoint presentation.

Following is a complete anecdote using one of these opening lines:

Harry, the leading rainmaker of a Century City law firm, wanted to retire and still receive his seven-figure income. Every day, the rest of the attorneys looked forward to the projects Harry would bring in, accumulating billable hours while sitting in their offices. Until one day, Harry came to work dressed in golf clothes and told everyone he was moving to Palm Springs. Because of that, the firm's partners huddled and, in a frenzy, sent out calls to recruit a marketing director. And because of that, I was brought in to energize the firm, from its website and collateral material to the staff's networking skills. Until finally, we had a contemporary brand, a freshly designed website, updated offices, and business communication training for all the partners and associates. Ever since that day, the rainmaking has been distributed among more of the attorneys, and profitability has increased.

APPLICATION

Every speaker must consider his or her audience when constructing a presentation. I am frequently asked how to appeal to those personality types with a short attention span (such as a CEO or an entrepreneur), while at the same time satisfying the rational ones (including a CFO, an engineer,

A well-told anecdote can satisfy people with both short- and long-term attention spans.

or a CPA) who need to delve deeply and understand how things work together before they are persuaded. A well-told anecdote is the answer.

Client anecdotes can open a presentation and let you immediately connect with your audience. They can be used as elevator speeches or to answer the question "What do you do?" Anecdotes are effective vehicles for explaining and bringing to life a technical point within the body of a presentation. If your presentation needs a more persuasive close, an anecdote is always a good choice. And anecdotes from your own experience are the best way to alleviate anxiety, exhibit what makes you different from your competitors, achieve buy-in, and ensure that your talk will be memorable.

6

Stage Fright

I was delivering a presentation on stage fright to a peer group of psychology professors at a national conference and asked how many get nervous when they speak in front of a group. About 40 percent raised their hands. These professors make their living lecturing to college students. I was surprised at the response, so I suggested an experiment. I told them that I would randomly select three volunteers to stand up in front of the assembled group and introduce themselves. To increase their anxiety, I said I wanted more than "Hi, my name is Peter, and I teach at Cal State University, specializing in stage fright." I told them that their introduction should be so compelling that at least three other professors would approach them afterward and ask for a lunch meeting. Then I said that after each speaker finished, the audience would be asked to critique his or her introduction to determine what listeners remembered and how much charisma the speaker displayed.

Everyone was instructed to make a few preparatory notes, since they all had an equal chance of being selected. When it was time to choose the volunteers, no one would make eye contact with me. They suddenly appeared fascinated with their shoes or the number of ceiling tiles. The tension was palpable. I quickly pointed this out and heard many nervous laughs. To heighten their anxiety, I made eye contact around the room and then paused. After two minutes of tension, I told them to relax; I wasn't going to call on anyone. But I asked them to write down what they were thinking and to predict what would have happened if they had been called on.

A few wrote that they had a good story to tell and were hoping to be called on, but more than 80 percent said they felt an intense sense of dread. The room was largely split into two camps. Members of one group were afraid they wouldn't be able to communicate well, that they would babble and sound inane. People in the other group said they could deliver the introduction but thought they would be judged as uninteresting. A few admitted that they developed a strong urge to leave the room before the selections were made.

No one should be surprised to hear that the fear of public speaking is the number-one fear for business professionals. To give you some perspective, fear of dying comes in at number five. Comedian Jerry Seinfeld said it best: "Remember the next time you're at a funeral that most people would rather be in the coffin than delivering the eulogy."

> Public speaking is the number-one fear for business professionals.

How intense is this fear? The U.S. Army performed insightful research to find a way to replicate the stress soldiers felt in actual combat conditions. They knew that when soldiers were frightened, neuropeptide Y hormones were released into their systems and depleted. The Army wanted to see how fast these hormones would return to normal levels to determine how effectively a solider would cope with battlefield stress. Researchers tried a number of conditions, like having soldiers stick their hands into a bucket of ice water, but none of the stressors mimicked battlefield conditions except one—asking soldiers to stand up and present a speech without preparation. Extemporaneous speaking turned out to be the highest stress inducer on the list. It was the closest thing to simulating the fear of actual battlefield conditions.

The best way to manage stage fright is to understand it. Stage fright results when a performer develops a fear of negative evaluation. In the next section, we break down the anatomy of stage fright into four stages so you can see how it develops and how to manage it.

THE STAGE FRIGHT CYCLE

Stage fright doesn't flip on like a switch. It starts with your thoughts and then grows the more you think about it, becoming a vicious cycle. Although the nature of each person's stage fright may

Stage fright occurs in four stages.

be different, the stages are the same. Notice how each thought is accelerated by the new evidence supporting it.

> George had recently been promoted to vice president of information technology in a branding and advertising firm. His rise through the company had been fairly rapid, based on his knowledge of technology, but his new position required presenting to various teams within and outside the company. Public speaking had never been an area of strength for George. In fact, he always tried to avoid it. He believed that people in advertising who pitch successful ad campaigns to clients, as well as to their own teams, would hold him to an even higher standard for communication.

Stage 1: Initial Predictions

We make predictions about everything we are about to do. This process is pervasive, even for the simplest of actions. If I am thinking about going into the kitchen for some milk and cookies, I still make several predictions. I believe there will be a container of gingersnaps in the cabinet and milk in the fridge to wash them down. Having faith in my predictions, I enter the kitchen. If I believed the snaps had gone soft or the milk had passed its expiration date, I would opt instead for a trip to the grocery store. This prediction process is so automatic that it is often below our radar, and we are rarely aware of it.

Whenever you are going to make a presentation, you make a prediction of how well you will do based on your knowledge of the content, how artfully you will deliver it, who will be in the audience, and how you judge your own speaking ability. When you experience stage fright, it means that your predictions about the outcome are negative.

> The process of predicting how things will turn out is automatic.

George had to make a presentation to the board of directors to convince them that large capital outlays were necessary to upgrade the company's IT equipment. He was afraid that IT was a low priority for management. As far as the presentation itself was concerned, he believed that he lacked the persuasive skills to convince the directors otherwise. He knew that he would be very nervous and it would show in obvious ways like sweating, dry mouth, flushed skin, and the inability to put a full sentence together. He thought his nervousness would be interpreted as incompetence by his listeners. He was also afraid that they were expecting a very slick presentation, and he would look like an amateur.

George predicted doom coming at him from several directions. Anxiety results when we believe that something bad will happen to us and we don't have the resources to cope with it. The anxiety is heightened when the outcome of the situation has important consequences. George created a lot of worries for himself. This is a classic example of a negative prediction.

Stage 2: Anxious Response

There is a simple formula for anxiety. When you believe something bad will happen and you can't cope, your body reacts to these thoughts with symptoms like a rapid heartbeat, shaking hands, sweating, red skin, and shallow breathing. Psychologists refer to these symptoms as indications of the "fight-or-flight response." When you believe you are in danger, you typically try to escape, and if you can't, you have to stay and fight. In either case, your heart pumps more blood to your extremities; you sweat to cool your body down; and your thinking becomes focused on survival. This is an efficient system—unless you are not really in mortal danger. Then these symptoms get in your way, especially during a presentation.

When you are speaking, your level of anxiety can make you feel either challenged or overwhelmed. When challenged, you are focused and present. You remain "in the moment." All distractions disappear, and your brain is firing on all cylinders with the sole aim of accomplishing your goals. When anxiety becomes severe, it spikes right past "challenged" and goes into "overwhelmed." When you are overwhelmed, your mind goes blank, and this interferes with accessing the material you know well and want to present. Your thoughts are consumed by survival.

If you are not in danger but *believe* you are, you can think yourself into a state of high anxiety. If you were terrified of spiders, saw a black spot out of the corner of your eye, and believed it was a spider, you would immediately panic. A few seconds later, you might notice that it was just a black button or piece of paper and breathe a huge sigh of relief, but during the time you thought you were in danger, you were scared. The relationship between thoughts and emotions is powerful.

> You can think yourself into a state of high anxiety.

Crossed Signals

You've invited Bill and Joan, a couple you recently met, to dinner. You put a great deal of thought and planning into the meal. Then you spend hours organizing and cleaning the house, deciding what to wear, and preparing the meal. Your expectations are high. At fifteen minutes past the time set for dinner, you tell yourself they are just being "fashionably late." When they are a half hour late and haven't called, you begin to question what's going on. Finally an hour has gone by, and they haven't shown up or called. Would that make you angry?

Most people say, "Yes, of course," but think again. It is your assessment of the intention behind their behavior that makes you angry, not what they've actually done. If you believe they had a better offer or just didn't care enough to remember your invitation, you will be upset—and rightfully so. The fact that Bill and Joan haven't shown up is not the issue. It is your *perception* that they are rude and inconsiderate that causes your anger and resentment.

Let's reconstruct the scene to see how you might react to a change in the story. Imagine that after an hour and a half you finally get a phone call from Joan. She tells you that as they were leaving an upscale wine shop, where they stopped to buy a bottle of wine as a gift for you, Bill slipped on a wet spot, hit his head on the ground, and was knocked unconscious. He was rushed by ambulance to the emergency room, and this is the first chance she's had to call you. He is still unconscious at the hospital. What would happen to your anger now? It would immediately evaporate! You might even feel embarrassed about having been angry at Bill and Joan. You would simply reevaluate the situation and revise your interpretation.

The key point is that you *think* yourself into emotional states; they don't just happen based on actual events.

Your next set of negative predictions is based on the thoughts you identified in stage 1 and the new evidence you have from your physical anxiety symptoms. When you begin thinking of all the things that could go wrong and how they would affect you, your body begins to respond with a faster heart rate, rapid breathing, sweaty palms—all the usual suspects. As you begin to experience these symptoms, you know there must be something serious to worry about or your body wouldn't be going haywire like this. Your predictions now induce an even greater anxiety, because these physical symptoms provide "proof" of how bad things really are.

Every time George thought about giving his talk, he began to feel anxious. He had trouble getting to sleep the night before the presentation, and on the big day, he was a walking mass of nerves. He knew this situation was dangerous and could seriously affect his career, or he wouldn't have felt so many symptoms. He believed that signs like these happened for a reason.

Stage 3: Self-Monitoring

Your brain is wired so that you can only perform one complex thinking task at a time. University of Michigan psychologist David Meyer puts it in perspective: "There is no free lunch. For all but the most routine tasks . . . it will take more time for the brain to switch among tasks than it would have to complete one and then turn to the other." You could easily carry on a conversation with a friend or write a letter on your computer, but you would find it very difficult to write a letter *while* you were carrying on a conversation. Meyer says, "Humans can eat lunch and read the paper at the same time, because eating scarcely involves conscious thought." So the only time a person can multitask without errors or dangerous results is when one or more of the tasks have become automatic. Clearly, public speaking is not automatic.

Distraction

The following cognitive science experiment explodes the myth of multitasking and explains one of the major causes of stage fright. Count the number of words in this sidebar. Not difficult, right? Now count them again, but this time, do it while you repeat the word *count* over and over. You probably found that repeating a simple word totally disrupted the equally simple task of counting. If repeating a single word can disrupt your concentration on a simple task, imagine what thinking about something frightening can do while you are trying to focus on something as difficult as your presentation.

This third stage is at the heart of stage fright. When you are giving a talk and begin to notice your physical symptoms or try to assess the audience's reaction, you divide your attention, and you cannot do that without paying a price. The more attention you assign to self-monitoring, the less you have for your talk. When you see a speaker stumble over content he knows well or have that deer-in-the-headlights look as he stares blankly at the audience, there is a strong possibility his attention is directed inward on how he is reacting to his physical symptoms; he is focused on self-monitoring.

David points out that actors are trained to direct their focus away from themselves and onto the interaction with the other actors. If an actor is performing and thinks, "I'm especially good tonight," there is a good chance that she will forget her lines. Similarly, if an actor thinks, "What if I forget my lines?" or "What if I blow this scene?" she becomes seriously distracted.

> Focusing on the physical manifestations of stage fright will only make matters worse.

These are a few examples of self-monitoring that turn thoughts into self-fulfilling prophecies. Because the brain can only handle one complex cognitive task at a time, when

In the Moment

Mihaly Cziksentmihaly is a psychologist noted for his work on the psychology of flow. In this state, you are fully engaged in what you are doing. You feel energized, focused, and totally free from distractions. You don't think about what you are doing—you simply do it. Your concentration is high, and your sense of time is distorted. You can totally lose yourself in what you are doing. At the same time, you are in the moment and keenly aware of all feedback, so you can react to it. Best of all, it feels great to be in a state of flow.

a speaker is truly in the moment, concentrating on how best to engage an audience and directing his attention outward, anxiety is reduced and he is much more likely to approach a state of flow.

> George began his presentation feeling very nervous. As he was speaking, he noticed the CFO and COO of the company laughing about something. He noticed someone else looking at her watch. He felt himself begin to sweat, and his heart felt like it was going to rip through his shirt.

Stage 4: Making Mistakes

If you continue to split your attention between your talk and the distraction of self-monitoring, the chances that you will make mistakes increase dramatically. It may just be a temporary groping for the next thing to say, creating a silence that you fill in with a few annoying "ums" or "you knows," which are distracting and incredibly nonpersuasive.

Or it may be more serious—blanking out and becoming confused. As you begin to have actual problems in your talk, they affect the next series of predictions you make. Now you have your initial predictions, physiological symptoms, divided attention, and a few actual problems on which to base subsequent predictions. This may spin some speakers completely out of control, and they remain seriously nervous throughout the remainder of their talk. We have seen speakers race through their remaining content or finish abruptly and walk off the platform just to stop the pain.

When George was in the middle of his talk, he began making small errors. As he became aware of them, he lost his place. As he attempted to click through to the next PowerPoint slide, his remote didn't work. He stumbled through the remainder of his presentation, superficially covering what he had wanted to say in detail, and ended his talk awkwardly and abruptly.

Self-monitoring is the presenter's biggest problem. But preparation and practice will allow you to manage it. Now that you know how stage fright comes about, it's useful to determine which of two types of stage fright you may be dealing with. They are not mutually exclusive; you can experience both.

> Prep and practice to diminish but not eliminate stage fright.

THE TWO TYPES OF STAGE FRIGHT: COMPETENCE AND ACCEPTANCE

Just as there are four stages of stage fright, there are also two fundamental types. The first deals with your ability to deliver your performance. One of the most common fears people have is forgetting what they are going to say. They are also afraid that they won't appear competent to their audience. Stage fright is situational. You may believe that you can explain something well—until your CEO or a nationally recognized expert sits down in the second row. For theater actors, when they see a knowledgeable critic in the audience, their stage fright is often activated.

The Face of Fear

I interviewed Paul Salomunovich, former music director and conductor of the Los Angeles Master Chorale, who told me this story. Years ago, Paul took his choir to Rome and performed before the pope, the entire college of cardinals, and about six thousand people in St. Peter's Square. He said it was fun, and he felt no fear whatsoever. Two months later, he took the same choir to Atlanta and performed the identical show in front of the American Choral Conductor's Convention. He said he was so nervous he could barely hold on to his baton.

Why would he be more nervous in front of a bunch of choral conductors than before the pope? Because here was little chance that the pope would notice if he missed the downbeat in measure 24 of the Bach cantata, but the choral conductors would be buzzing about it for months.

The second type of stage fright has to do with how accepted you feel by the audience. You may be enormously competent and do a great job delivering your presentation, but will the audience be impressed, amused, or persuaded? I had a colleague who taught at the university with me for thirty years, and he was nervous every time he stepped in front of his class. He was brilliant and clearly knew much more about psychology than his students, but he thought they found him boring. Just about every professional comedian goes through what's called "flop sweat" each time he or she goes on stage. Comedians never know if they are going to get laughs or not. They have all bombed. This is one of the reasons we caution you *not* to tell jokes.

PERCEPTION VERSUS REALITY

When presenting in front of an audience, there is often a gap between perception and reality. Unless you are a classically trained performer, your perception is that any emphasis, change of tone, or physical gesture is of much greater magnitude than it actually is.

When Deborah and David work with clients, they do an exercise called Taking Risks. Each individual is assigned a role as different from his or her personality as possible (such as having someone shy be a motivational speaker, assigning someone powerful and influential to be an insecure young person, or having an engineer play a bad Las Vegas entertainer). The clients present content using the language and behavior of that character.

The trainers encourage participants to exaggerate their behavior, play, and risk venturing outside their comfort zones. The exercise is recorded, and interestingly enough, when the DVD is played back, a typical comment is, "I thought I was over the top, but in reality, it's not that much different from how I usually present." Comments from the group back up this reality, not the speaker's original perception. The group often says the participant was looser and more engaging. Consistently, he or she appeared to be enjoying the experience and exhibited a high level of commitment. Our thinking has us believe that any change outside the norm is huge, when typically it is quite small. The barometer for judging our performance is calibrated incorrectly. Our perception has conquered reality.

> Your perception of your presentation, while you're giving it, is usually at odds with reality.

There is another factor at play. Our sense of time is distorted. A two-second pause can feel like an eternity, because time is so highly compressed when we are in a slightly anxious state. When you're speaking and all eyes are on you, your perception of *any* silence is magnified. Pause to breathe and gather your thoughts. A pause is exactly what you need at that moment to relieve the pressure, think on your feet, and demon-

> Occasional pauses are good for the presenter and for the audience.

strate confidence rather than racing or stumbling through your text.

In addition, a pause creates contours in your phrasing and is an effective way to create transitions. In spite of the way it feels to you internally, your listeners appreciate a pause because it allows them to digest the material you've just presented. It also signifies that you are a thoughtful speaker who is confident in your ability to engage the audience. The real benefit is that once you are back into your rhythms, stage fright is diminished.

PREDICT THE MAGNITUDE

Stage fright is not an inborn trait that some have and others don't. It arises based on the situation, and under the right circumstances, everyone will experience it. You can predict how much stage fright to anticipate for any presentation by considering two things: (1) your expectation of how you think you will perform, and (2) how much you have riding on the outcome, whether actual or imagined.

Daryl was a financial planner who relocated to Atlanta. Within a few weeks, he was asked to make two presentations:

When his son's seventh-grade teacher found out what Daryl did, she asked him to come in and talk to her economics class. Daryl agreed and gave a very relaxed and interactive presentation. Looking at the two predictive factors, Daryl believed he knew more about financial planning than any of the seventh-graders in the audience. He was sure he could answer their questions and also knew that if his talk was not well received, there would be few negative consequences.

Compare that to his professional situation:

His new company asked Daryl to make a presentation to the local Rotary club with three hundred active members. The company's CFO was the newly elected chapter president, and most of the top executives were also members. Daryl knew there would be many potential clients in the audience. Worse still, he knew there would be several people who had more experience in the field than he did, and it was made clear that this was his coming-out party. If he did well, he would generate a great deal of new business, and if he did poorly, it could take years to undo the damage. Not surprisingly, Daryl was quite nervous preparing and delivering this talk.

WRESTLING THE BEAR

There are three ways you can deal with stage fright:

- Performing relaxation and visualization exercises
- Reframing or shifting your perspective
- Changing your behavior

Managing Anxiety

Unpleasant emotions are at the heart of stage fright. Because your thoughts are largely responsible for your emotional states, you cannot directly control your emotions. Fortunately, you can put yourself into a state of relaxation. Eloqui tells their clients that a mild case of stage fright will keep them focused and make sure all synapses are firing. The trick is to manage the anxiety associated with stage fright. You have to ride the horse, not let it ride you. Relaxation and breathing exercises perform two vital functions: (1) they calm you down by lowering your heart rate; and (2) they oxygenate your brain, which increases your alertness and capacity to perform.

> Manage stage fright with relaxation exercises, a shift in perspective, and a change in behavior.

Here are some relaxation and breathing exercises that can help you manage nervousness.

Breathing Exercise 1. Sit and stare at one spot in front of you and begin to take slow, deep breaths. Inhale through your nose, hold the breath a few seconds, and exhale slowly through your nose. While you do this, focus your attention on your breath, concentrating on filling up your diaphragm and lungs and then slowly exhaling. You can do this exercise up until the time you begin speaking. Taking in air through your nose gently massages your cranial nerves, producing a soothing effect. An in-depth treatment of relaxation techniques is provided in my stage fright book, *Speaking Scared, Sounding Good*.

Breathing Exercise 2. This effective yoga breath exercise slows a rapid heart rate. Cover one nostril with your fourth and fifth fingers. Breathe in through the other nostril for a count of five. Hold for a count of five. Release your fingers; use your thumb on the same hand to close the other nostril, and breathe out for a count of ten. Breathe in through that same nostril for a count of five. Hold for a count of five. Release your thumb; use your fourth and fifth fingers on the same hand to close the other nostril, and breathe out for a count of ten. Alternate by closing first one nostril and then the other. When you can do it without shortness of breath, increase by one to a sequence of six, six, and twelve, and then seven, seven, and fourteen. Notice how your heart rate returns to normal and your voice drops to a lower register.

Imagery. In addition to relaxation and breathing techniques, you can use imagery to improve your focus and collect yourself. David trains sense memory, a useful anxiety reducing technique he learned from Sanford Meisner at the Neighborhood Playhouse Acting School in New York.

First, choose the one emotion, characteristic, or trait that will serve you best. For example, during a talk you may want to exhibit confidence, calm, empathy, or authority. A few days prior to the talk, find a quiet space to sit, uncross your arms and legs, close your eyes, and recall an incident or event where you exhibited or felt this particular characteristic or trait. Focus on all the details and sensory images surrounding that specific event. For example, what time of day was it? What was the temperature? What did the environment look like? What were you wearing? What sounds did you hear? Were there any smells? How did you feel physically? Were your muscles contracted or loose? What was going on with your voice, your gut, and your hands? While recreating that moment, squeeze your wrist. Then, approximately ten minutes prior to your speaking engagement, find a quiet spot, close your eyes, squeeze your wrist again, and recall a snapshot of that incident to quickly elicit the corresponding characteristic or trait.

There are variations on this technique when relaxation is your goal. One is to think of images and scenes you find relaxing and focus on them. Waves rolling onto the shore and lush meadows are common favorites. As you create an image, try to involve as many senses as possible to immerse yourself in the scene. In addition to just picturing a sunny beach, smell the saltwater, feel the warm ocean breeze or the sand running through your toes, and hear the waves breaking on the shore.

The other way to use imagery is to picture yourself performing with great success. Boxers visualize themselves pounding their opponents; musicians imagine themselves playing their instruments flawlessly and hearing the audience gasp. Speakers can picture an audience responding to their stories by nodding, laughing, or applauding vigorously. They can imagine future clients asking them out to lunch and placing a contract in their hands.

> Use all of your senses during your relaxation exercises.

In his book *Mind Wide Open*, Steven Johnson recommends basking in the success of a past incident or event. Many Eloqui clients have difficulty embracing this idea when it comes to speaking. Even though they have delivered a great presentation, elevator speech, or client acknowledgment, they focus on the *one* point they forgot, worry over why someone left the room, or beat themselves up for not being perfect. They have been taught to diminish their accomplishments and to set the bar higher for their next presentation. However, whatever you dwell on—be it success or perceived failure—will be the first memory that surfaces when you are facing your next presentation. Why not bask in a memory of success to make it more likely you will repeat it?

Creative Visualizations. David has shared that performers use a number of techniques to bolster their performance and place themselves fully in character. The following imagery exercises from acting schools will enhance your rehearsals and make sure that you are more focused and present when you are delivering your next presentation.

> Exercises derived from acting academies allow you to relax and be successful when delivering your next presentation.

■ **Grounding:** For some people, anxiety creates a dissociative feeling that can exhibit itself as light-headedness or an out-of-body state. To remedy this feeling, sit in a quiet place with your feet planted firmly on the ground, hands on your thighs, and eyes closed. Visualize your body as an oak tree and your feet as roots growing into the earth, giving you weight and substance. Breathe deeply, and on the exhalation, imagine the roots traveling deeper into the ground. After two to three minutes, you should feel calm and solid, offsetting the lightheaded, dissociative quality that stage fright creates.

■ **Golden orb:** This exercise counteracts the uncomfortable sensation created by having all eyes on you and gives you a physical metaphor for directing your energy and attention onto the audience. Sit in a quiet place before your presentation, and close your eyes. Imagine a small, golden orb in the center of your being, radiating beams of light outward. The ball grows larger with each exhalation, until it permeates your entire being and gives you a feeling of warm, soothing energy.

Note: the previous two exercises demonstrate that without a doubt, we are from California.

Breath Support. When experiencing anxiety, speakers often forget to breathe. If you are feeling a lack of oxygen, particularly at the beginning of a presentation and immediately after each sentence, take in mini-breaths through your mouth. When you have a longer pause, take in a larger inhalation through your nose.

While this quick method will help you in the short run, shallow breathing is inadequate to deliver extended sentences. Diaphragmatic breathing—making your stomach expand by breathing into your navel—is like filling a bagpipe and will give you enough oxygen for entire arcs of thought and projection. Women were always told to suck in their stomachs, which can result in shortness of breath, especially when they have speaker anxiety. Diaphragmatic breathing is practiced by opera singers, actors, and musicians. Practice this technique until it feels comfortable. It will help you relax and also improve your delivery.

Physical Warm-Up. Performers and athletes know the advantage of lessening anxiety and accumulated muscle tension through physical activity. Speakers who engage in their favorite sport or exercise prior to their talk will calm their nerves, clear their heads, and deliver more oxygen to their brains. If you still feel tight or stiff, vigorously shake out your muscles, especially your arms and hands to reduce tension in your neck and shoulders. Think of the swimmer Michael

Phelps standing on the blocks before a race at the Olympics. His long arms shook off anxiety like a flag in a strong breeze.

The same applies to warming up your voice, which is greatly affected by anxiety. Under stress, the vocal cords will constrict, forcing your voice higher or tighter. When your mouth is dry, it's difficult to form words and enunciate clearly, which can be unnerving. On the way to your presentation, while walking or driving, gently warm up your voice by humming *m*'s and *z*'s.

Shifting Your Perspective by Changing Your Thinking

The second point of attack for dealing with stage fright is to shift your perspective. If you've ever been depressed and tried to tell yourself to cheer up, you know how difficult—if not impossible—it is. With stage fright, you focus more on negative than positive thoughts as a survival instinct. If your back hurts and your arm does not, you pay attention to your back or you might injure it further. Unfortunately, this leads to some bad thinking habits that creates logical fallacies and often increases stage fright. Here are a few logical fallacies resulting from negative thinking.

Overgeneralizing. William received a few hostile questions from clients during a presentation he made on marketing strategies. He is now worried that this will occur every time he gives a talk. By taking one instance of a bad event and being perpetually frightened about it, he has overgeneralized his fear and raised the likelihood of increasing his stage fright in the future.

Maximizing/Minimizing. Jeri sold group medical insurance. She went out on a series of eight presentations in two weeks. She did really well in seven of them. The last one didn't go so well, and Jeri focused on only that one. She didn't acknowledge the other seven good presentations and felt like a failure because of one poor outcome. This tendency to maximize failures and minimize successes

Men Versus Women

This is where men and women approach the problem differently. In Eloqui seminars, the male perspective is often expressed as "How bad can it be? They're not going to shoot me if I totally mess up," which he considers an effective way to adjust his thinking. On the other hand, women generally feel anxious for days before a presentation, concerned that they don't know enough and they will be judged harshly by the audience or client, so they tend to exaggerate negative consequences.

prevents a balanced evaluation of your performance. It makes it difficult for you to determine where you need work and what elements are successful and should be kept and emphasized.

Begin by identifying your fear-provoking predictions and then see if there is any real evidence to support them. If not, learn to shift your perspective and change your thoughts. For example, one of the most common fears is blanking out during a presentation. People are terrified that they will forget what they are supposed to say and end up staring mutely at the audience. Challenge yourself by asking if there is any evidence of such a meltdown in your past.

> Stage fright is often based on assumptions we make about ourselves that have no basis in reality.

If you realize that such an event has never happened, it is easier to change your belief that such an event may occur in the future.

However, if there are fear-provoking thoughts that *are* based on evidence, you will have to work harder to build up skills in those areas. For example, if you have actually blanked out while speaking, you should organize your talk as thoroughly as possible, speak in venues with a lower ante, or develop a system to remember content. For example, rather than memorizing your talk, construct an outline with bullet points. Use large fonts and/or a highlighter so you can glance down and easily retrieve your content. Include trigger words or phrases that indicate a story or example you wish to relate. If necessary, also include transitions.

For long lists of talking points, consider a mnemonic, assigning a letter to each point that together spells out a word that is easy to remember. For example, the following "points" form the word *object*. *O* = *obstacle* client was facing. *B* = *breakdown* in communication. *J* = *job* we did to overcome the problem. *E* = the way we *excelled*. *C* = the *cost* of doing business. And *T* = the *transformation*. Speakers can write up the mnemonic on a page or two or place each point on a note card. Do not ever write out your complete text but give yourself trigger words, phrases, or examples that support your mnemonic and keep you on track.

Changing Your Behavior

The easiest way to attack stage fright is by changing your behavior, which is directly under your control. Robert worked for a major financial firm that forced him to use its prepared PowerPoint slides to avoid deviating from the company message. Robert hated speaking and experienced major anxiety each time he had to give this presentation. He also wasn't successful in obtaining new clients from his talks, undoubtedly because his delivery was flat and his demeanor lacked vitality and enthusiasm, due in large part to his stage fright.

Robert came to Eloqui to get the tools to be a more dynamic speaker. But that wasn't the issue. The problem was the restriction created by the PowerPoint presentation and believing he had no options. What was in his control was the verbal presentation. Deborah and David interviewed Robert to find client anecdotes and examples to liven up each slide. They also directed him to give the audience one primary takeaway per slide. Now Robert could breeze through the morass of graphs and charts. He found a way to be in control, both of his presentation and his stage fright. Not surprisingly, his anxiety diminished, his presentations became much more persuasive, and the seminars were a venue for attracting new clients.

TECHNIQUES FROM THE ENTERTAINMENT INDUSTRY

Choosing a role (such as the mobilizer, trusted advisor, or facilitator) is another way to change your behavior. It is not only effective for delivering a persuasive presentation, but it also reduces anxiety. A role establishes parameters, dictates how to frame your content, and eases your burden; it's something over which you have control. When speakers experience anxiety, they typically fall back on their default mode, which means they speak faster, deliver more data, ramble or repeat themselves. Once you select a role, you feel grounded and find it easier to stay in the moment; you can fall back on the parameters of that role rather than on your own default mode. (See Chapter 2 for more on roles.)

A role gives you the security of speaking from behind a mask. As a director, Deborah was used to being in charge of the cast and crew of a production, but she became nervous when speaking in public. By assuming the role of facilitator, she put her full attention on the audience, made her presentations interactive, and used the "mask" of the facilitator to diminish her anxiety. For example, if she was asked to speak on how to develop business through networking, she would ask for volunteers. Rather than lecture, she worked with each volunteer on his or her elevator speech and then polled the audience about what worked and what didn't. By choosing the role of facilitator, focusing on a specific task, and encouraging audience participation, Deborah considerably reduced her anxiety and became a more effective and persuasive presenter.

> Assuming a role can reduce anxiety.

Given Circumstances

Prior to the curtain going up in a theater performance, David reduced anxiety by practicing "given circumstances." This technique walks a character through the events that lead up to the present moment. The actor imagines himself as the character waking up in the morning. He remembers what clothes he put on, what he ate for breakfast, and the first person he encountered. He continues walking through the events of the day and considers how these events have affected his character. This serves two important functions: (1) it gets the actor in touch with his role, and (2) it reduces performance anxiety.

Actors are also trained to eliminate distractions prior to performing. They learn to release their concerns about events of the day. By creating a neutral mental space, there is room to infuse their character with given circumstances. Actors call this process "bridging," or transitioning from their personal life to that of the character.

Speakers also need to prepare for their role. Ten minutes before your presentation, bridge from whatever activity you were involved in to the focused role of a speaker. You'll need to eliminate all distractions, either by writing them down or asking an associate to handle them. Then find a quiet space, even if it's in the restroom. Practice one of the relaxation exercises described earlier in this chapter, and focus on your breathing. Deborah's favorite mantra just prior to speaking is "They need what I have to deliver." Once your thinking is clear, recall your intention, or objective, for speaking and envision yourself being successful. Now you are ready to go.

> Presenters, like actors, should eliminate all distractions prior to speaking.

One Eloqui client has written a number of books on doing business in foreign countries. Lynn is called on to address business groups and political appointees. She is frequently seated among guests and potential clients, chatting sociably during lunch. At the appointed time, she is asked to stand and address the group as the keynote speaker. Until she learned to bridge by excusing herself, finding a quiet space, and shifting into speaker mode, the openings to her talks were awkward and lacked focus.

Rehearsal Gold

One of the best ways to reduce stage fright is through practice. Many people procrastinate and avoid rehearsal because it is stressful.

Frequency. The flip side is, if you over-rehearse, your performance has a good chance of becoming stale. The trick is not to rehearse your presentation the same way again and again. When you use the same wording each time, your brain begins to memorize the text, and most of the life is drained out of the delivery. Rote rehearsals equal rote, dull performances. The irony is that frequent practice can *prevent* stale performances if done correctly.

Map out an outline of where you will travel with your presentation. Craft the opening and closing and identify the main talking points. Select anecdotes or examples for each of those points. Then during rehearsal, vary the way you deliver the presentation, using different wording or phrases each time. This type of rehearsal will not only increase your grasp of the subject, but maintain the integrity and energy of your presentation. The goal is to never memorize your presentation but to have a solid grasp of the outline, leaving room for improvisation and audience participation.

> Practice not only refines your presentations, but it also reduces nervousness.

When you are in command of your material, it frees you up to be in the moment, because you are not hindered by trying to remember what to say next. If a waiter drops a tray during your talk, you are asked a question, or the decision maker at the table says, "I just received an important call. Can you wrap it up?" you will have no trouble incorporating these disruptions into your presentation if you've rehearsed it properly.

Close to Reality. There is an abundance of research showing that you will perform better if you practice under performance conditions. This is referred to as "state-dependent learning." For example, reading your notes is helpful, but it is *not* practicing. You need to say the words aloud.

Also, before you deliver a presentation, it is essential to find out as much as possible about the physical conditions to minimize surprises and the resulting anxiety. Ask your contact or personally check out the following:

▪ **How many people will be attending your presentation?** Although a larger audience creates a more formal atmosphere and can affect the way you address the group, there is really no reason to be more formal in a larger space. You *will* need to expand your gestures so that you occupy more space physically and vocally, but that's the only difference. Convey the same personal, relaxed, informal feel that you project in smaller venues. To do that, imagine sitting across from your audience at the dining room or conference table.

▪ **Will there be a microphone and amplification?** If there will be a PA system and you will be using a microphone, practice with one. Find out if it will be on a stand or podium or if it will be handheld. Wireless microphones include headset mikes or lavalier mikes attached to part of your clothing. If that is the case, you should dress appropriately so there is a convenient place for it.

If you are in a large room, without amplification, you should practice using a loud voice. Imagine that you are addressing the person in the farthest corner of the space. It feels different to give an address in a soft voice than to project to the back of the room.

That difference can cause you a great deal of discomfort if you didn't prepare for it.

▪ **Will you be introduced?** If someone will be introducing you, you must determine if you need to write your own intro or if he or she will write it for you. Regardless of who will be delivering your introduction, determine what information you think the audience will find useful or colorful.

▪ **Will you be sitting at a table, standing behind a podium, or free to walk around?** Delivering a presentation has a very different feel depending on whether you are sitting, standing, or pacing. Find out the arrangement and practice that way.

▪ **What are the incidentals and details?** If you rarely wear a suit and tie, or heels and a skirt, then dress as you will for the presentation when you practice. We have seen performers fuss with a starched shirt and tie while they talked, because they were not used to wearing them. Practice walking up to the podium, putting your notes down and adjusting the microphone to your height. The more familiar you are with your speaking environment and the process, the fewer surprises will distract you.

Distraction Training

Distractions lead to internal thoughts that can throw you off during a presentation. Practice being distracted and getting back on track. Work at identifying where you left off each time and then continue. This will give you confidence. At the famous Moscow Art Theatre, Konstantin Stanislavsky had two students present a scene while the rest of the class ran around them, screaming and waving their arms. When the actors went on stage for the actual performance, they felt bulletproof.

Directors encourage actors to rehearse their opening lines out loud. The same holds true of speakers. Both can be so focused on the enormity of the project that they look beyond the opening and blow their first few lines, which results in extreme anxiety. Rehearsing the opening, in particular, allows actors and speakers to warm up their voices so that they're naturally placed in the center of their vocal range. Researchers have determined that the greatest amount of anxiety occurs during the two minutes before you go on and the first two minutes of your presentation. The more you have rehearsed your opening with various interpretations, the better it will be, counteracting the effects of peak-level anxiety.

> Practice distractions to reduce your level of stage fright.

Accustom Yourself

During a few practice sessions, stop and run in place for a minute or two until you get slightly out of breath, your heart rate increases, and your palms get sweaty. These are the same physiological symptoms that you have when you experience anxiety. Practicing while you feel these symptoms will prepare you to perform if (or when) anxiety arises on the platform. Replicate the actual presentation conditions as closely as possible.

Expect the Unexpected

For most of us, being prepared and knowing what is expected of us reduces anxiety. However, surprises can create havoc for speakers, especially in the most vulnerable first few minutes. Seldom does a presentation come off the way you've planned it. What would you do if the audience member you were most trying to impress left the room just as you were introduced? What would you do if the PA system went down, or the wait staff served the meal just as you started talking?

Deborah and David attended a presentation given by a client at the Friar's Club in Los Angeles. The speaker, Donald, brought along his own technician, who didn't have the right connector to hook up his laptop, which ran the PowerPoint presentation, to the club's older-style projector. While the lights were dimmed, Donald tried to direct the technician's efforts rather than address the audience and take control of the situation. He needed to step out from behind the podium, deliver his talk, and gain the audience's admiration, showing that he was able to surmount the difficulties. Instead, the audience was unsettled because Donald drew their attention to the problem and his own escalating discomfort.

> Replicate physical anxiety symptoms while you rehearse.

AUTHENTICITY

The greatest anxiety producer Deborah and David see with their business clients is the speakers' perception that they need to be someone else when delivering an important presentation. There is a belief that they need to be more authoritative, more formal, and less emotional. Incorporating their own perspective has historically been considered "soft" or inappropriate. All of the speakers' unique traits, characteristics, and interpersonal skills are subjugated in an attempt to be seen as professional.

Times have changed. These misguided assumptions create a serious disconnect, a total separation between business and personal lives.

James is a man who by any standard would be considered exceptionally powerful and wealthy. He has exerted a considerable influence in business circles, run large organizations, and turned around three savings and loans. He was even responsible for naming a suburb outside Los Angeles.

> To reduce stage fright, just be yourself!

He has sat on boards of international corporations and functioned as a president, CEO, and, in his early years, second-in-command to two of the world's wealthiest individuals. James is also an engaging, natural storyteller.

Yet when all three of his daughters were married, he was unable to stand up and honor them or give a simple toast because of stage fright. Why? James had set the bar too high and felt that, because of his position, people expected him to say something of great importance each time he spoke. Three priceless moments were lost forever.

Six months ago, at his parents' funeral, James was initially glued to his seat and unable to express his love and sense of loss for the two people he held most dear. But James refused to let anxiety win. Haltingly in the beginning, he stood up and expressed himself simply, clearly, and from the heart—without affectation. When you have an important presentation, being yourself is probably the single best way to combat stage fright.

7

Presenting in Teams

W atching the debacle of the 2008 U.S. Olympic men's and women's teams in the 4 × 100 meter relays in track and field was painful but instructive. Both teams were brimming with medal and world-record holders, and they were favorites to win the gold. However, neither team even qualified for the finals. Their Achilles heel was the handoff of the baton, a seemingly insignificant transfer of a hunk of pipe. These world champions failed to recognize the importance of working together as a team, believing the race was only about individual raw speed and power. But without the finesse of an effective handoff and the connection and cooperation between team members, they experienced the agony of defeat and watched others savor the thrill of victory.

Both American teams made adjustments, rehearsed passing the baton, and won gold in the next two relay races. But what they had lost could never be retrieved.

Athletes are not the only ones who are slow to respond or who experience failure before reexamining their process. Following are ten dumb things we've seen smart companies do to lose team pitches.

1. Spending the majority of prep time compiling the content for the pitch and little or none rehearsing the delivery or handoffs
2. Having the most senior person in the firm deliver the majority of the presentation
3. Failing to look at the presentation as a team production that warrants finesse and orchestration of individual parts
4. Bringing along associates and junior staff who sit mutely at the table or nearby, while a senior staff member delivers the presentation
5. Leaving out why this particular team was assembled and what specific talents each person brings to the table
6. Disregarding the need to appoint a facilitator to drive the agenda, sense the client's engagement, direct comments, and elicit questions
7. Opening the pitch by describing the services and experience of your company in great detail
8. Constructing PowerPoint slides or a "pitch book" (a researched, in-depth description of the proposal, potential outcomes, and company background) to serve as a cuing device and reading nearly word for word to ensure that nothing is left out
9. Allowing anyone who is not currently speaking to stare at and assess the reaction of the client
10. Failing to support all team members by not giving them assigned roles, cutting them off, or disagreeing with their comments

Typically, team presenting is thought of as multiple speakers, each taking their turn to present a section of content, or as one person driving the majority of a pitch with minimal participation from the other individuals in attendance. Neither of these scenarios qualifies. True team presenting mirrors everyday conversation, when we bounce ideas and concepts off each other. It is closer to a dialogue than a series of monologues.

Yet like a conversation where someone steps on another's comments, overtalks, interrupts, or fails to be a good listener, team presenting done poorly can lose business.

We find that the most successful method of team presenting comes from the world of ensemble acting. Like any good stage production, working in an ensemble has untold benefits and enhances the performance of each team member.

> Working as an ensemble will make your team—and the individuals on the team—successful.

THE BENEFITS OF TEAMS

Recently, Eloqui pitched a major financial services firm to train their executives in communication skills. After spending less than thirty minutes with Frank, the key decision maker, he stopped the interview and told us, "You're hired." When we asked why, he said, "You model the behavior we want our executives to demonstrate, especially the way you two present and hand off."

When asked for specifics, Frank was more definitive. "When one of you finishes, the other picks it up; you even complete each other's sentences. You listen intently and complement each other. I believe you know your content and will deliver what you promise." He was making a decision based on observing the verbal *and* nonverbal execution of team presenting techniques.

When you present as a team, the audience listens to each individual but takes in much more. Listeners observe *how* you work together. When your handoffs are smooth, when you demonstrate that you like and respect each other, and when each of you has a clearly defined role, your audience can't help but generalize that you do business the same way.

Presenting in teams has enormous advantages. When two or more individuals deliver a presentation, it reflects the depth of experience within their company. As each team member demonstrates his or her competence, it illustrates that every aspect of a project will be handled well. Team presenting can also exhibit how well staff members work together and complement each other. The harmony they project is perceived as the harmony that their organization can create within the client's company.

> Presenting as a team can project the image of a harmonious organization.

Another advantage of team presentations is that younger, less experienced associates can partner with senior-level executives, giving the former an opportunity to observe, learn, and bring their own talents to the table. Team presenting is an excellent way to groom bright, young professionals for advancement. Newer associates have often conducted much of the research and analysis on a project. They can make compelling arguments and support the experienced team members. Everyone wins. Senior staff exhibit the patina of credibility gained through experience; youth also has its own advantages. Many technology-based companies have been founded and run by

> Presenting as a team is a way to highlight up-and-coming talent in your organization.

young entrepreneurs who often trust the research, trend indicators, and predictions of their peers, more than those of the gray-haired executives who make up many investment banking or financial firms. Having team members of various ages overcomes this chronological divide. Your thoughtful selection of team participants demonstrates that you understand the task at hand and can match appropriate resources to best serve the client's needs.

Finally, presenting in teams creates far less anxiety for everyone concerned. When there is a clear division of labor and each member only needs to be concerned with his or her role, it frees up valuable time and energy; people don't need to be worried or anxious about elements of the business that other team members have already mastered. The resulting presentation will require less preparation for each participant and ensure that the team as a whole is more effective and successful.

COMMON MISSTEPS AND POTHOLES

Over the years, Eloqui has seen a great deal of team presenting that is awkwardly conceived, poorly executed, and ineffective. In the late 1990s, we witnessed a pitch given by IBM. A senior executive, Michael, came in to make the presentation, followed by ten additional staff, all in similar dark suits, white shirts, and striped ties. While Michael talked, the others sat and nodded but did not speak. Why were they there? Why didn't they say anything? What message did this convey to the client?

The IBM scenario is not uncommon. In a team presentation, it's typical for the CEO or seasoned executive within the firm to do most of the talking. This occurs even though the CEO usually does not have the most knowledge about the project and is frequently unfamiliar with the details. Other members of the team sit quietly, while the potential client directs all questions to the person who is speaking. Some companies think that if their senior executive *isn't* the one making the presentation, it will show a lack of respect. The belief is that by featuring the CEO, it demonstrates the weight given to the project, even if the chief executive isn't the most qualified person to make the presentation. Sometimes it is the ego of the CEO that won't allow others to share the spotlight.

To make matters worse, since the responsibility of delivering the presentation falls on the senior-level executive, he or she often has to rely heavily on a pitch book or PowerPoint presentation that someone else has prepared. It's not surprising that after the pitch, if the firm lands the project, the only person the client will deal with is the individual who led the presentation.

> Having a CEO present alone is often the worst decision your company can make.

Eloqui is often called on by that weary executive whose plate is now too full. She is unable to delegate the project to her staff because of the expectations *she* has set. Unfortunately, it's difficult to change the perception that has now been built into the project.

The CEO or senior executive has become the point person, and the client will be disappointed, and often even insulted, if anyone else is brought in as a substitute. Because she did most of the talking, she is seen as the key contact and the *only* one to deal with. If it is a matter of respect with one of your clients, have your CEO be part of the team, but let the ones who are most qualified carry the major parts of the presentation. That way, they are immediately identified as the team members with whom the client will actually be doing business.

One investment banking firm that contracted Eloqui had the reputation of being the most technically competent in its field. The company was known to garner the highest sales price for its clients and possessed the strongest support staff of analysts and associates. However, the firm too often lost pitches to less capable competitors. It made no sense until we uncovered the format of the investment banking firm's presentations.

After cursory introductions, the managing director, Larry, began going through the prepared pitch book, one page at a time. The book allayed his fear that he would be asked a question he couldn't answer. It also showed a high level of preparation. But by remaining tied to a prepared presentation, Larry left little room for the client to participate. The price Larry paid for his security was a lack of interactivity and a monologue—an often dreary one at that—instead of a dialogue.

When you mechanically go through a pitch book or PowerPoint presentation, you create obstacles to engaging clients and other team members. For example, if the owners of a company are considering selling their firm, it is an emotional decision. They really want to talk about it. They are seeking an investment banking firm that listens to their struggles, understands their history, and supports the legacy they wish to leave behind. It is this personal connection that often means as much to an entrepreneur as the numbers. Larry came to understand that his investment banking firm had lost sight of this, believing that his company's technical expertise and track record would be sufficient to win business.

But it's important to note that dividing content among members of a team doesn't necessarily ensure any more interactivity than having one person make the entire presentation. The process can *still* sound like a lecture and fail to leave room for dialogue. The participants may not listen well to one another or to the client. There needs to be a concerted effort to ask questions, listen to the responses, and incorporate those answers into the presentation.

> Simply dividing speaking responsibilities among team members is not enough.

WHAT'S AT STAKE?

When law, architectural, accounting, investment banking, and even product manufacturing firms compete for an important project, they often send teams. There is a lot riding on the outcome. Substantial fees, commissions, expanding ongoing relationships, the potential for new clients, and the enhancement of a company's reputation all create enormous pressure.

It's amazing how much time, effort, and money is expended on developing the content of a pitch, while the delivery of the material is ignored or, at best, relegated far down the list of important prep items. When Eloqui began training team members of Larry's investment banking firm, we asked how long they spent researching and assembling a pitch book for upcoming presentations. They told us that, on average, it takes about three weeks. When we asked them how much time they spent rehearsing the actual presentation, they said, "On the plane—sometimes." In most businesses, rarely do teams rehearse to maximize their effectiveness or prepare for contingencies, distractions, or emergencies. Yet experience has taught us that a team's language, division of roles, and interaction are stronger factors in being awarded a contract than the actual content of the proposal.

When the field is narrowed to the top players and you are a finalist bidding on a project, there is often little difference between you and your competitors. If your product or services weren't exceptional, you wouldn't be on the short list. It's similar to the U.S. relay teams. On paper, the teams were separated by only hundredths or thousandths of a second. So they focused on speed, which was unlikely to improve that late in the game. They failed to focus on what could have improved—the handoff. In the same way, many organizations fail to focus on the one thing that can set them apart from the other viable candidates: the team presentation.

CONFIDENCE IS SEXY

A vital element for team presenting is confidence, which can be reinforced and bolstered between the participants. When pitching a potential client, you have to believe you will win. The question becomes, with similar credentials and expertise, how can your company truly differentiate itself? Or put another way, what is your unique ability to deliver a product or services? We've had potential clients come right out and say, "Why you?" Having a ready answer that you deliver with confidence will set you apart and be a critical factor in your success.

In business pitches, we see fundamental flaws in the way most teams prepare. The selected participants are well qualified and know their information, but they doggedly assemble and review their content in isolation. Their objective is to do a good job with their specific section. There is little emphasis on how the parts fit together and how the ensemble will perform. Partners often overlook

> In a team presentation, the whole should be greater than the sum of its parts.

the opportunity to build the strength of the team by complimenting one another on their specific skills and the value this delivers to the client. To exhibit confidence in a team presentation, the whole should be greater than the sum of its parts. The perceived impression of your team is every bit as important as the content you deliver.

COMPOSING SUCCESSFUL TEAMS

Think of the last panel of experts you observed. Sometimes a host is assigned to moderate the discussion in an effort to keep it moving. One after another, individuals talk for a set period of time. Sitting in the audience, you probably make a mental assessment of how many speakers there are and how long it will take for each one to speak.

Compare this construction to a string quartet. Can you imagine if the first violinist played his part solo, then the cellist played her part, and so on until every member of the quartet finished, bowed, and left the stage? As in music, we are attracted to counterpoint. Mini-presentations are simply more engaging than listening to one person speak for a long period of time. The purpose is to maintain the client's interest and attention.

Unpredictability is compelling in a presentation. If you divide your presentation into two equal segments, recited in sequence by two team members, the audience can easily get bored. Conversely, if the topics are handed off multiple times, the interaction keeps the audience engaged. It is more dynamic to bounce an idea from one team member to another. You create interest and stay ahead of your audience. Interaction inevitably reveals different perspectives, including what the audience or client is thinking.

> Dialogue among individual team members is more engaging than listening to one person for a long time.

A well-written string quartet depends on the interplay of the performers. They all play in harmony with one other. Each part is written with the others in mind. The same is true of an effective team presentation. For example, the facilitator drives the agenda and makes sure that whenever the client has something to say, the pitch team pauses to hear him. The technical expert addresses her area of expertise. When one person is talking, the others watch supportively and listen to make sure all key points are covered. Another team member may run a laptop or write on a white board for whoever is speaking. The key is that *everyone* has a role during every minute of the presentation—and it all has structure. Like creating music, there are principles for composing a team presentation.

How Many Is Too Many?

Our client at Mattel told us that when a lot is riding on a presentation to the buyer at Wal-Mart, Mattel will assemble anywhere from three to eighteen people to make the pitch! Is it any wonder that the Wal-Mart buyer gives each person only thirty seconds to deliver his or her report and the Mattel team is anxious?

The ideal configuration in any team presentation is two, or at the most three, individuals. When your team is composed of two people, one can assume the big picture role (such as the mobilizer, trusted advisor, or visionary) and the other can be the detail or process person (the facilitator or liaison). Sometimes we hear from our clients that they need to bring a technical expert along to serve their clients best. (See Chapter 2 for more details on roles.) If you believe bringing additional presenters is essential to your success, we won't argue. However, in our experience, this scenario is rare and dilutes the effectiveness of the team. In addition, assembling large teams is not the best use of participants' time, especially those who do not need to be in the meeting.

Identifying the Objective

The initial step to a successful team pitch is identifying a shared intention. If a car were stuck in the mud, you wouldn't have one person pushing it from the front and another pushing it from the rear with equal force. In the same way, you don't want team members to pull their audience or client in different directions.

Without a common objective, each person feels compelled to include everything he or she possibly can to land the potential client. Individuals with their own intention may end up competing with their colleagues for recognition, advancement, or status. And without a *shared* intention, the presentation lacks focus and can be perceived as fragmented.

Team presentations are *not* about the needs of each speaker to be center stage. Take a field trip to a local Guitar Center or any store that caters to rock musicians. You will see several teens playing guitars. Worse still, you will hear and feel them. One will thrash around at an ear-splitting volume that stimulates the next kid to outdo him. As each one pumps up the volume, the result for everyone in the store is a mixture of cacophony and pain. Presentations with competing objectives are similar to this scenario. You do not want each team member trying to outshine the others. Whether it's playing louder or trying to sound more competent, effective team members don't dominate—they collaborate. While three competing teens can drive you deaf and angry, one hundred orchestra members can be exhilarating because of the way they play together.

> The team must have a shared intention.

Key Roles and Players

A pianist does not play with the string quartet unless there is a part written specifically for her. You may have a competent staff, but that doesn't mean they should all participate in a particular presentation. Once the shared objective is determined, a well-functioning team identifies key participants based on their experience with the client and their knowledge of the information germane to the presentation. Once the team has been selected, roles need to be assigned.

For example, an investment banking firm has an initial meeting scheduled with a CEO who is considering selling his company. There are two ways to handle this presentation: send an individual or a team. If the firm chooses to send an individual, it would make sense to send a trusted advisor who is at a similar level to the CEO. He can discuss both big picture and process, and share observations gleaned from his own experience. The informal meeting would serve the purpose of information gathering, build an ongoing relationship, and lay the foundation for further talks.

By contrast, the investment banking firm could send a team of two individuals. One would be responsible for the big picture. He would speak from his experience, ask questions, and envision the possibilities. However, he would bring along a facilitator to describe the details, day-to-day responsibilities, and the mechanics of selling the CEO's company.

In this case, the investment banking firm decided to send only the big picture person or trusted advisor for the first meeting. Thomas was concerned that bringing someone else along could perhaps stifle the CEO's ability to open up and share his feelings about selling his company.

To reinforce a casual approach, Thomas wore a polo shirt instead of the traditional white shirt, blue or red tie, and dark suit. The men met over a cup of coffee. Thomas made the desired connection with the CEO, who asked for his advice. Thomas recommended a second meeting where a handpicked team would present the parameters of the sale process. The two developed a strong relationship that eventually led to Thomas's investment banking firm and team selling the CEO's company.

The All-Important Facilitator

This person introduces your team when everyone first enters the room. A proper introduction tells the clients why each member of the team was assembled *specifically for them*. Introductions are also a sign of consideration, so clients don't wonder who the players are. Also, it is more effective for the facilitator to showcase everyone else. She can heap praise on a colleague that would sound arrogant if he expressed it about himself. Introductions should include

> The facilitator should explain why each member of the team was chosen specifically for the client.

members' strengths and what role they will serve in the meeting and eventual project.

Eloqui is sometimes asked if the big picture person should make introductions and take the lead. There are no hard-and-fast rules about orchestrating a presentation. Base your decisions on the culture of the company you are pitching (e.g., is it hierarchical, male dominated, or youth oriented), the relationship of the participants, and the abilities of your team members.

For example, perhaps a younger associate or sales rep has built a relationship with a member of the potential firm. In that case, he would facilitate. Perhaps the CEO, founder, or managing partner has decided to lead the team, making the pitch for symbolic reasons; she would cover the purpose of the meeting and why this team was selected. Or perhaps someone is simply more skilled in facilitating meetings and making compelling introductions, so that person is best suited for the facilitator role. This individual should also have a finger on the pulse of the client's reactions. When there is or may be a question, it is the facilitator's job to make sure that question is thoroughly addressed.

The facilitator is essential for keeping the meeting on track and making sure the team achieves its objective. Strange things can happen to people when they get in the spotlight. Some become deer in the headlights and need rescuing. Others become hogs and need nudging off the stage. Still others become disoriented. It is the facilitator who politely stops someone from rambling with a humorous comment such as, "Jill is so excited about the possibilities for your project, she may never let Bill show his slides," or "Bob loves numbers so much that if we let him go on like this, you'll all earn three units of CPE credit."

If the facilitator senses restlessness in the room or a lack of engagement, it is his job to deal with it. There are several ways to handle this. He can ask a question. He can present an assumption such as, "Maybe we haven't sufficiently addressed Steve's point about valuation. Is there something we missed?" or, "I'd like to go off script now and make sure we're covering what's important to you."

Often, a client starts to speak or ask a question, but the presenter is on a roll and doesn't stop to acknowledge it. When that happens, the facilitator must stop whatever is happening *immediately*. Inexperienced presenters will talk over the client because they are following a prescribed plan. This is a big mistake. Presenters must check their egos at the door and let the client or other team members speak when there is an overlap. It is the facilitator who makes sure this essential task gets done.

A very common complaint of business executives is that presenters do not listen. This is a compelling reason why vendors are not selected. More than any other technique for team presenting, the ability to listen to one other and to the client will give you the greatest result. When you actively cue and listen to clients you are able to incorporate their wishes or concerns into your presentation. As our law clients tell us, many trials are won or lost because of the way the jury *feels* about a lawyer or a witness. A decision can be traced directly to how much an audience likes you. Listen and answer your clients thoughtfully and with respect.

> The facilitator should make sure the client's questions are answered immediately.

Physical Positioning

When Peter began studying graphic design and page layout, he learned a very important principle. You can take a graphic element and dump it anywhere on a page, but as soon as you have two elements, you need to create a *relationship* between them. One must be aligned to the other, however creatively you do it. Similarly, when two people present together, you have to create a physical relationship between them. You must determine the distance between them, their orientation toward the client, and what space they occupy.

The distance between people conveys important clues about how much they like each other and how well they work together. In the

United States, the preferred distance between standing individuals is roughly an arm's length apart. Any closer and they will crowd each other. Much farther and it looks like they don't care for one other.

As one person speaks, the other should angle her body to face the speaker, with both leaving their chests slightly open to the audience. Imagine an inverted triangle with the point between the two-person team, or said another way, standing at a forty-five-degree angle to one another. This physical proximity and relationship says, "We are presenting as a unit, not just occupying the same space." If the listening presenter stands or sits in profile, facing the speaking presenter, this signals that the speaker will continue for a longer time, and the listener becomes invisible.

Once you've mastered the easy stance together and would like to be more dramatic, practice moving with your partner. Sometimes a presenter is more dynamic or kinetic; standing in one place feels unnatural. When one of you wants to make an important point and crosses in front of your partner (downstage toward your audience), your partner needs to cross behind you, taking your original position, to avoid being blocked by you and to keep the triangle intact. The goal is to end up on the same plane next to each other. It's similar to playing doubles tennis, when you move to the other side of the court to cover a greater area. Both players must move in sync. In theater, this move is called a countercross.

> For frequent handoffs, stand to form an inverted triangle.

We are often asked how to position team members when they are seated. Rather than take positions on either side of the table, which forces the client to ping-pong their gaze back and forth, we recommend that the participants sit next to one other on the *same* side of the table or around the corner from one other. Since the tendency is to watch the individuals who are *not* talking, as well as the speaker, the client can easily make an assessment of how engaged the listeners are when team members are seated together. The proximity to one another also implies collegiality and cooperation.

HANDOFF TECHNIQUES

We opened this chapter with the story of the 2008 U.S. relay teams. The key to winning a closely matched race is how smoothly one runner can pass the baton to the next runner on the team. When one speaker stops and the next one begins, that is a handoff. Instead of a baton, the audience's attention is redirected so they are barely aware of the transition. With fluid handoff technique, you don't have to structure your presentation so one individual after another speaks for a predetermined length of time.

The U.S. track coaches said they didn't have much time to practice handoffs prior to the race. Not only do corporate teams fail to practice handoffs, most aren't aware of handoffs as a separate skill that they should or even *can* practice. Consequently, they frequently drop the baton. Here are key skills to the art of the handoff.

Cue with Your Voice

Traditionally, if you wanted your presentation partner to speak, you looked or gestured to her or asked her outright to take over. After two or three times, this method of passing the baton looks like a bad vaudeville routine or the "throw" among local TV news anchors. It's clumsy and obvious.

First, be clear about completing your thought. This will provide a conceptual segue or transition. At the same time, signal your teammate with your voice. When you want him to pick up the conversation, use a downward inflection, conclude your statement, and put a definite period at the end of your phrase or sentence. Trust that your teammate will pick up the presentation without you having to gesture, nod, or ask. Once you have put a period at the end of your sentence, pause briefly so that the other presenter can pick up the cue. If you speak in run-on sentences, use an even or upward inflection, or never fully end a thought, it is impossible for a teammate to speak without interrupting you. You are not giving him a clear signal that it is his turn.

Here is the secret that makes for a seamless handoff. The speaker needs to finish her thought by putting a downward inflection at the end of her statement while looking out at the audience. Although tempting, she should not turn to look at the next person speaking *until* she hears his voice.

> Signal a handoff by using your voice, not a gesture.

Most people think that to slow the pace of a presentation, you would intuitively speak slower; conversely, to speed up the presentation, speak more quickly. Wrong. Allow a longer pause when a speaker finishes to relax the pace of the presentation. To pick up the pace and energy of the presentation, leave no pause and have the next person jump in as soon as the speaker finishes. Actors call this "tightening a cue."

Since cues are so important to the perception of a well-oiled pitch machine, what do you do when your partner finishes and you have no idea what to say? Borrow a technique from improvisational theater called the law of agreement. This is different than simply saying, "I agree," or "That's right, Susan." Reinforce or repeat the last word, phrase, or idea your partner expressed. The intent is to buy you enough time to build on the

> After handing off to a partner, do not look at him or her until *after* he or she has started speaking.

concept and move the conversation forward. If you're totally stumped, repeat only the last phrase or idea, deliver a downward inflection, and trust that your partner will jump back in.

HOW TO DISAGREE

Another question posed to us is what to do if you disagree with your partner. This can be tricky, especially since you want to demonstrate how well you work as a team. However, if you believe that your partner's comments could be damaging or negatively affect the outcome of the presentation, there are options. First, to show your respect, you can say, "Fred has experienced this situation from his position. However, in my department, we see it this way . . ." The idea is not to make Fred wrong, but to offer an alternative opinion that is equally valid. A slight variation may be, "Fred has experienced this situation, but you may have experienced it differently. We are open to a discussion."

What you don't want to do is put up roadblocks to the dialogue. Another aspect of the law of agreement is the concept of "Yes, and . . ." versus "No, but . . ." When you openly disagree with your partner, you are, in effect, ending the conversation.

> When disagreeing with your copresenter, use "Yes, and . . ." rather than "No, but . . ."

Try it with a friend or colleague. Discuss a subject with no emotional heat to it. For example, debate whether it is better to shop for clothes at the mall or online. You'll notice that when you emphatically disagree and make the other person wrong, the conversation ends. However, you can use the technique of "Yes, and . . ."; for example, "With Mary's busy schedule, I can see why she shops online. For me, I need to try on clothes to make sure they fit and reduce the time and money of returning items." Now you've given your partner a way to build on your comments, even though you disagree.

GLUED TO THE SPEAKER

Whenever you are in second chair (listening), your job is to give support and look directly at the speaker. In this way, you are engineering assent in the room. Listening team members should nod, smile, or, when asked, add a complementary opinion. The purpose is to convey the perception that the team works well together and to direct positive energy throughout the room.

> Look at your partner when he or she is speaking.

Believing they are invisible, listening team members have been known to take notes, look around the room, or consider what they want to say next and not focus on the speaker. Nonspeakers may be accustomed to looking at the clients and assessing their reactions. These actions are what actors call "pulling focus," or drawing attention to themselves and away from the presenter. Trust that the speaker is making the necessary eye contact and gauging the client's reaction. That's his or her job.

By watching the speaker carefully, it will become easier to tell when she is about to finish. Conversely, when *you* are speaking, remember to include your partner in your eye line, looking at him occasionally. Give him as much eye contact as if he were a person in your audience. If your audience is small, you will look at your partner frequently. If your audience is large, once in a while is sufficient.

In addition, when you keep team members in your range of vision, you can tell when one of them wants to contribute to the conversation. Agree on signals ahead of time for cuing your partners. For example, if you want to say something, you might lean toward the speaker, open your mouth slightly, or widen your eyes when she looks at you.

> Occasionally make eye contact with your teammates while you are speaking.

DRAMATIC TENSION

Never underestimate the nonverbal cues that telegraph how your team operates. A potential client will be watching all of the participants, not just the individual who is speaking. What will the client see?

If presenters are awkward with each other, interrupt, look away, or act disinterested while other team members are speaking, the potential client takes this as indicative of the way they work. The client will observe their behavior in *this* environment and assume it is the way they would behave if contracted for a project.

The British playwright Harold Pinter pointed out that audiences enjoy drama; they are instinctively attracted to it. It doesn't have to be logical, and they don't have to know what led up to it—they just want drama. If you were at a concert, and the man and woman sitting next to you began hissing at each other in low voices and jostling with their elbows, you would watch. You would be captivated even though you didn't know if they were married, dating, or in business together. You would watch because it was dramatic. And you would fill in the gaps and make your own interpretations about what was happening. The key point is that it would hold your interest.

With this in mind, if you saw two team members disagreeing and giving each other dirty looks, or if a younger team member looked intimidated and stopped talking midsentence when an older team member interrupted, you would fill in the gaps, and your perception would not be positive. Audiences or clients watch anything that catches their interest. Make sure what they see is what you intend them to see.

TOTAL TEAM CHOREOGRAPHY

Consider team presenting a performance, with each of the players connected to each other while being acutely aware of the client. Also, like a performance, the pacing, momentum, and cue pickup contribute to the overall integrity of the presentation.

Practice Makes Prefect

To learn handoffs, begin by choosing appropriate roles. Then, rehearse with the actual material for your upcoming meeting, session, or pitch. Take a section of the presentation and practice handing off to your teammates. Teams can change and get reconfigured, so team members need to be flexible and easily incorporate new players. One Eloqui client travels to many cities and picks up a local representative before each presentation. He then does what he refers to as "parking lot train-

> Handoff techniques can be learned quickly.

Name This Dysfunction

Eloqui was in the process of renaming our business, which was once called David Booth Associates. At that time, we happened to draw the winning ticket in a contest sponsored by a marketing firm and won a free consultation. We were excited, because the timing seemed so ideal. At the meeting, we filled out all the forms and anxiously awaited the presentation by the firm's two partners, John and Dena, who were joined by Maggie, the director of marketing. The meeting was closer to a theatrical farce than a creative brainstorming session. Dena and Maggie clearly didn't get along.

When Dena spoke, Maggie would interrupt and disagree with her. When Maggie spoke, Dena would roll her eyes. Maggie moved close to us, leaving her teammates hugging the back wall. On occasion, John would make a grand gesture or statement, trying to cover up the "cat fight" going on around him. It was a disaster and made us very uncomfortable.

A week later, John followed up with a phone call to see if we wanted to do business with his firm. There was no way we would work with them. Their internal relationships made them look totally dysfunctional. John asked for feedback, and it was diplomatically but directly given. Unknowingly, this opened a Pandora's box. At first, John was astounded that we could tell anything was wrong. Then he confided to us that they were having problems and considering letting Maggie go. He asked if we would meet with the three of them and facilitate a discussion to reach a resolution. We respectfully told him that group therapy was more in order.

ing." Joe claims he can teach team presenting skills to a new partner in the parking lot in about thirty minutes before a pitch.

Practice handoffs to become familiar with how your teammates respond. At first, exaggerate the downward inflection signifying you have completed your thought. Then make it subtler until you feel confident that your partners know when to pick up their cue. With sound technique in place, you can be nimble and comfortable because you know your partner has your back.

The methods are not difficult to learn, nor do they take much time to incorporate into your own shorthand. The positive impression they deliver, however, is enormous.

Another way to keep the presentation engaging is to vary the length of material delivered by each person. Start out with brief opening statements, then have one person go into greater depth or take a longer section. But keep it conversational. Even when one person has a lot to deliver, other participants should stay involved by asking questions the client might ask or cuing the speaker to tell an anecdote that demonstrates her point. When your team is transitioning to another topic, a quick back-and-forth repartee will liven up the presentation. As in music, variety and unpredictability keep the client's attention.

Presentations are full of uncertainty. You need to know that you can count on your teammates and create successful handoffs when necessary. Plan on allergies kicking in, your throat drying up, your brain blanking out on a section of your material, the PowerPoint failing, and many other things that require flexibility and nimble behavior. Mastering handoff techniques will allow you to enter any pitch or presentation with the confidence that your team is prepared for any circumstance.

> Variety and unpredictability keep the client's attention.

Emotionally Engaged

We work with an architectural design firm that often presents in teams. Individually, they are all bright, intelligent, enthusiastic professionals. But the minute they were placed together on a team, it was as if someone had drained the life out of them. A sense of formality pervaded each presentation. They addressed each other in a robotic fashion that seemed to say, "We work together because we have to." They didn't keep eye contact with each other. One by one, they followed a prescribed script of presenting their content.

After videotaping a mock pitch, we gave them our reaction to their presentation style and choices. Rather than sugarcoating it with niceties, we were blunt. Eloqui has found that mock presentations reveal the same mistakes or habits that people demonstrate in real presentations or pitches. Flattering our clients would not assist them in changing. We told them their delivery was tepid, their energy was sleepy, and they each delivered their own content with little regard for how it linked to the team effort. Even though it was a mock presentation, they failed to ask questions of the potential client or assess the client's needs and concerns.

The CEO told us we weren't the first to give them this feedback. So we probed for specifics. They said it was their impression that designers and architects had to act knowledgeably, professionally, and with authority to be taken seriously. They were afraid that if they were too enthusiastic, the potential client would think they were creative types—or, even worse, salespeople.

We recommended a total reversal to let their clients know why they were passionate about their business. We encouraged them to ask questions and make assumptions, even if those assumptions were wrong. Now it was up to them to take the risk and bring their personalities forward.

Six months later, the architectural design firm pitched a major player in the technology field who wanted to expand its U.S. footprint by building an entire campus in San Jose, California. Our architectural firm competed with entrenched heavyweights from the Bay Area. Instead of a static presentation, they invited the technology company to visit their completed projects. The architect and project manager assumed big picture and detail roles and used subtle handoffs as they walked the potential clients through the buildings. They followed the advice of

Let your passion show in team presentations.

writer Lillian Hellman: "Don't let the stitching show." It didn't seem like a pitch at all. Showing off their actual work brought out their enthusiasm, focused on the visuals, and triggered great dialogue. The architectural firm landed the business, which was their largest project to date.

Team presentations should not be a series of boring recitations. Ideally, they contain interaction, emotional persuasion, and opportunities to compliment and feature your teammates. Conversational dialogue is far superior to delivering professional-sounding, canned speeches one after another. Clients want to be engaged and know that you share their passion.

Since it is within your control to engineer assent in the room, be positive and support your teammates unequivocally. Always rehearse the delivery and handoffs, as well as the content. Whenever possible, digitally record your practice presentation. Then watch it as if you were the potential audience or client to appreciate what they will see. Make adjustments and have the confidence that you are now prepared to win. With these simple precepts to effective team presenting, you will no doubt increase your success rate. And like the 2008 U.S. Olympic teams, practice *all* the mechanics, so when you return for the next race, you can win the gold and set world records.

8

Physical Grammar

Movement as Punctuation

hris Rock related in a television interview that as a young comic, he would plant himself behind the microphone and never move. One night, his idol, Eddie Murphy, was in the audience. After the show, Eddie recommended to Chris that he incorporate movement into his routine. Eddie mentioned that early in his own career, he'd noticed that the audiences in clubs would look away and talk during his jokes, which really frustrated him. But he figured out that the audience assumed he would be in the same position whenever they stopped talking and looked up. To keep their attention, he began to pace back and forth during the jokes. It worked. Chris took Eddie's advice and is now in constant motion, not only bleeding off nervous energy, but forcing the audience to pay attention and focus on him.

Movement arouses the central nervous system. Notice what happens when you watch TV or read. You often begin to feel drowsy. Watching a boring, static speaker behind a podium also produces drowsiness. In relaxation exercises and hypnosis, the first thing psychologists do is ask the subject to stare at one fixed spot. As a speaker, this is not the way you want to become hypnotic. In response to the traditional mode of standing behind a podium or being trapped next to a PowerPoint screen, Eloqui devised a system of movement to support and punctuate the spoken word. We call this system Physical Grammar because it is the physical equivalent of commas, periods, pauses, and exclamation points when speaking.

> As a presenter, you attract attention when you move.

Being mammals, our eyes follow movement. This is a primal survival trait. Fortunately, as a presenter, you attract attention when you move. The audience can't help but watch. Conversely, when you move and then stop, the sudden absence of movement is compelling and creates emphasis.

THEATRICAL BLOCKING

Movement in the hands of a well-trained actor is a powerfully expressive tool. When I performed in the theater, the moment I entered a scene, I knew I could deliver the character's sense of self-absorption, attention to detail, confidence or fear, aggressiveness or cowardice, desire for contact, or any number of subtle emotions or traits through movement alone.

Movements should have a purpose that supports what you say. When I was hired as a theater director, one of my first tasks after casting the talent was to block the play. Blocking is sketching out where and why the actors move. The *why* is important, because the purpose of movement is to illuminate the text in the script, while illustrating the personalities, needs, and traits of the characters. This is what we call "justified movement." Blocking keeps the production dynamic and, if done well, never draws attention to the movement itself. Transitioning from being a classically trained actor to a director, I understood the fundamental architecture of blocking and the behavioral impulses that dictate why one character would approach or avoid contact with another.

However, there is another world of nonverbal language that can be delivered to an audience. With blocking, a director controls audience members' focus by directing their attention to a point on stage through the action of the characters. Giving actors expressive moves that match the script enhances line readings and increases the impact of the words. This "symphony of energy" created from nonverbal clues connects listeners to the scene, plays on their emotions, and gives credibility to the piece.

A word of caution: In the final week of a three- or four-week rehearsal period for a stage play, if I want to shake the actors out of complacency or flat line readings, I change the blocking. We're not talking about a big move—just a little cross to the right instead of the left or standing instead of sitting. I can successfully predict that this simple change of direction will cause actors to forget (or dry up on) their lines and become confused. So as you decide to incorporate the various movements in this chapter for your next presentation, take heed. Incorporate only one move at a time so you are not thrown off and forget your content!

> If you are adding or changing movement to your presentation, do it one manageable piece at a time.

CLASSIC MOVES

The rules of physical movement within a space have changed little since the classical Greek theater twenty-five hundred years ago. Congruity between word and movement informs the audience. Movement illuminates the text and enlarges the presence of the speaker as she controls the space instead of being trapped behind a podium or seated stiffly at a table. The following movements should be incorporated into your own style and used *only* when you feel the impulse to punctuate a phrase, sentence, or thought. That is the formula for the art of effective movement.

> **Stage Directions**
>
> The directions "stage left" and "stage right" refer to speakers' or actors' left or right as they face an audience. *Upstage* and *downstage* are theater terms now in common usage. Upstage is away from the audience; downstage is toward them. The derivation of *upstage* is from the ancient Greek theater when it is thought that slaves would rake dirt uphill toward the back of the stage. This created an inclined plane (also called a raked stage) so that taller actors did not block the sight line of audience members in the front rows. In today's parlance, the word *upstaging* has a negative connotation. When two people present or are on stage together, and one draws the audience's focus by moving upstage of the other, she is upstaging her partner because the audience sees mostly his back.

Speaker Moves

The tendency of untrained speakers is to move indiscriminately. It's generally not something they think about or are even aware of. For example, some people rock back and forth when they speak, while others remain completely still and wooden. Unjustified movements and repetitive gestures draw the focus of the audience away from the message. Lean and economical movement keeps the focus on the message, so this kind of movement is always preferable.

Overcoming Bad Habits

Many of our clients feel vulnerable when speaking in front of an audience, which results in covering up their vital areas, as when hands are clasped across the lower abdomen or even lower (called the "fig leaf"). Some men are prone to taking the military stance, with feet shoulder-width apart and hands clasped behind them. The old dictum for men was to gesture with only one hand at a time and leave the other in a pocket. Since it was considered poor form to gesture with both hands, we often see men who leave both their hands in their pockets throughout their presentation. Other speakers have received critical comments for using their hands too much. The telltale sign is when they grip their hands together to keep them from moving. However, it always appears odd when you intentionally keep your hands together rather than releasing them to gesture freely. Instead, begin by letting your arms hang loosely at your sides. It may seem awkward at first, but resist the urge to put your hands anywhere else. Within seconds of speaking, you will begin to use your hands, because they are free and ready to gesture.

When speakers are truly engaged, they use their hands, and their gestures support and complement their content. It's nearly impossible to talk without your hands and be really expressive. In his groundbreaking book *Telling Lies* (which is the basis for the TV series "Lie to Me"), author Paul Ekman says that people illustrate or use gestures to punctuate their words because they have emotional investment in what is being said. Conversely, when someone is lying and carefully monitoring his or her words, there are few gestures or illustrators. When speaking, it's important to note that there is no right or wrong way to use your hands. Do whatever feels natural for you. The only caveat is that if you employ a repetitive gesture, like counting on one hand or pointing, be aware that your audience will notice it. The movement itself attracts listeners' attention and draws focus away from your message.

> Begin with your arms loose and at your sides during a presentation, ready to gesture.

Political candidates have been schooled in the use of nonaggressive gestures. Reviewing old videos, I noticed that in the mid-1960s, candidates stopped pointing at the audience and folded back one finger to lessen the intensity. It looks a bit odd, and you only saw politicians and some corporate executives doing it. In today's political arena, the pointing is often replaced with fingers pressed tightly together in an open hand that looks like it's about to break wooden boards in half. This is also odd and unnatural. Open your hands and gesture naturally, without a constricted grip; people will only notice the punctuation you give, not the design of your gesture.

Physical Neutral

I taught as a guest artist in acting conservatories, where "physical neutral" is defined as standing comfortably, feet shoulder-width apart, and hands at your sides. To achieve this state of neutrality, the actor must wipe the slate clean of any personal tics or mannerisms and *replace* them with the physical demeanor of their character. There should be nothing to distract the audience from the character.

Before you speak, stand in physical neutral. (Many women prefer standing in ballet's fourth position, with one foot turned slightly out. Feel free to stand like this if it feels more natural.) A solid stance makes you open and accessible to your audience, without a defensive posture or signals. Without anomalies to draw their focus, your listeners' attention is on your face. They hear your message without distraction. Beginning in physical neutral also allows you to move easily in any direction and open up to the audience.

To stand in physical neutral, imagine a point in the center of your chest and draw it forward slightly, allowing your shoulders and midsection to open. Uncross your legs and arms. Take your hands out of your pockets or from behind your back. Make this your rest position. This neutral stance also telegraphs confidence and enables you to use your hands easily to express yourself. Being physically open and available encourages the audience or client to embrace your ideas.

> Being physically open allows the audience or client to embrace your ideas.

Theme

Your theme represents the "whole idea." It signifies the central, driving force behind any presentation. At the beginning of ancient Greek plays, the head of the chorus walked to the center of the stage and explained to the audience what the play was about. That convention still resonates with audiences today. When you introduce or revisit your theme, move to the center of the available space, however it is configured. The central idea equates to the center of the space. This is another way in which congruity of idea and placement reinforce one another.

> Move to the center of the space when introducing or revisiting your theme.

The Exclamation Point

When you want to make an important point, a natural inclination is to move toward the audience. In actuality, the most effective move is to cross downstage on an angle toward your audience. This dynamic move bisects two planes and breaks through the invisible fourth wall of the stage. To put an exclamation point on your statement, cross energetically, add a pause or more vocal power, and include a gesture so the importance is accentuated. Since both the movement and statement are dynamic, you have now doubled the effect on the audience.

There is no specific rule of thumb about how to execute a downstage cross. Do what feels right. You can walk, stop, and talk. Or you can begin a comment, cross, and then finish your statement. The strongest use of this device is to end the movement at the same time you finish your statement. Plant both feet at the end of your

> When you want to make an important point, move downstage toward your audience.

cross. Make sure your heel is not off the ground and your toes are not up. A partially executed move signals indecisiveness. Also remember that distance is relative. One step in a small space can be as emphatic as a long cross in a large space.

Once you have executed a cross and find yourself downstage, there are a couple of ways to return upstage. Practice a "button hook." While keeping your chest open and making eye contact with the audience, make a semicircle, walking upstage center in the space. Or, if you know the distance from your current position to the back of the space, walk upstage while facing the audience.

Think Along with the Speaker

If you are posing multiple questions or ideas, walk back and forth parallel to the audience, and stop at the end of the series. This lateral movement says, "Consider these points," or "Think along with me." Maintain eye contact with the audience and proceed at a measured pace so this movement isn't interpreted as distracting or pacing like a caged animal. If you want to punctuate a list emphatically, stop before the last point, pause, and then deliver the final item. The absence of motion has drawn the focus to you and your closing idea.

> Walking back and forth across the stage invites the audience to "think along with you."

Differentiating Topics with Space

Audiences understand different topics or geographical areas if you delineate them using different areas of your stage. At an Amgen national sales meeting, one of the vice presidents gave a report on the domestic and foreign markets. He talked about the United States while standing stage left and then moved to stage right to talk about Asia. The audience saw each market more clearly as he moved between them because they were visually distinct.

Similarly, if you wish to enhance a transition, move to a different area of the stage; you literally create distance from the last statement or idea. Your next topic will appear fresh.

Creating Intimacy

Moving directly downstage toward the audience in a straight line can be seen as intimidating or aggressive. But the perception completely shifts if you lower your voice and move slowly as you approach your listeners. In this way, you create an aside. Moving closer to the audience signifies a need to share something personal or intimate. At the Thousand Oaks Civic Center speaker series, Tom Brokaw delivered a talk from behind the podium about his illustrious career as the anchor of the "NBC Nightly News." But when he wanted to share a more intimate story, he walked to the side of the podium and leaned against it. That small move took away the barrier of the podium and made him appear closer to the audience. Interestingly enough, when he returned behind the podium, he depended on his notes and lost some of the connection he had established with the audience.

> Cross to a different part of the stage to introduce a new idea.

Using this kind of movement to enhance the intimate connection between the speaker and the audience works anywhere. When all her kids left for college, Deborah's mother, Mickey, went back to work running a temporary employment agency. The local high school principal asked her to come and talk to the student body about secretarial work during the summer.

The family lived on the South Side of Chicago, and the high school was mostly composed of tough kids and gang members. Mickey wasn't shy, but she was not imposing at four foot eleven, and like most people, she dreaded speaking in public. However, she knew that standing behind the podium would be like driving her Pontiac; behind the wheel, people could barely see her. Her solution was to walk to the edge of the stage and sit down. Mickey broke the invisible fourth wall and eliminated the distance between herself and the students. She overcame what could have been a huge impediment, instead creating a vivid picture of self-assuredness, with her short legs dangling over the edge of the stage. She let everyone know who was boss while giving them strategies to get ahead.

INCORPORATING MOVEMENT

Here is an interesting paradox: You should only use physical movement that feels natural to you so it appears authentic to your audience, *and* you need to learn to use the physical movement techniques in this chapter so you can incorporate them into your presentations for greater effectiveness.

Donald, a financial titan, was preparing for a national media tour. After reviewing tapes of his recent interviews, he observed that he came across as stiff and uncomfortable on television. Over the years, he had trained himself to exhibit "no affect" in high-stakes business pitches. Like a good poker player, he never revealed a "tell." Although this served him well in business negotiations, it was a detriment on camera.

Donald watched news anchor Brian Williams and analyzed Brian's precise posture and gestures. One of the things Donald observed was that when listening to his guests, Brian tilted his head twenty degrees to the left. Because Donald was trained as an engineer, he applied this formula to his own behavior. It took weeks of Eloqui coaching to convince Donald to listen intently to the interviewer, treat the encounter like a conversation or friendly dialogue, and open up emotionally to exhibit authenticity instead of applying a formula. Rather than tilting his head or imitating someone else's gestures, Donald needed to trust that by connecting with the interviewer, he would be effective and the right moves would naturally follow.

Take one example of physical movement described in this chapter and try it out in front of a mirror. Experiment with it in a small, nonintrusive way and then in a big, exaggerated fashion. Try to *feel* how this affects what you are saying. If it makes your point more forcefully, begin using it. Expect to practice a move many times until it is comfortable. Physical skills have to be rehearsed until they get into your muscle memory and feel natural. If you took a tennis lesson and learned a new way to hit a backhand, you wouldn't expect it to be perfect the first time. It takes practice and familiarization.

You can also learn from the media. Start watching comics doing stand-up or one-person shows. Observe how great dramatic actors on TV and film take command of their space and punctuate their words with their bodies. If the performer is good, chances are you don't notice her movement as separate from her words. But each movement has been carefully chosen to bolster the meaning and importance of the dialogue.

Think of your actions as amplifiers for your words. They make your message clear and precise. If you have the opportunity, record yourself practicing and see if there is congruence between content and movement. Does it look the way it feels? When you are being watched by other people, everything can seem magnified. Time slows down, and it is hard to speak. It is also difficult to recall precisely how you delivered a talk. But a video or DVD recording is purely objective. Studying yourself on camera allows you to better assess how you appear to your audience or client.

Learning to use movement effectively is an essential step but not the final one. Incorporating movement as part of your ongoing communication is the way you make it your own. There is a reason movements signify transitions, exclamation points, themes, and so on. Your job is to discover how they punctuate *your* message.

I can always tell when people are new to using PowerPoint. They employ every bell and whistle available. They use too many font colors, highlights, clip art, fly-ins, and builds simply because they can. Keep this cautionary example in mind, and apply the new body language tools you've learned sparingly. Just because you can punctuate a statement with movement doesn't mean you have

Use movement sparingly and effectively.

to. Reserve these tools for the really important points you want to make. You don't have to cross the platform for every phrase you want to emphasize. Save movements until you feel the impulse to clarify or punctuate your ideas, then they will be most effective. For example, when opening a presentation, stay in one place for the first couple of minutes so that the audience or client will focus only on you and your message.

THE CODA

The same rule applies to closing your entire presentation. Hold your ground and stay in one place for maximum verbal impact. Any movement will diminish the importance of your final words. The greatest jazz musicians know when *not* to play.

Ending a Section

If you want to clearly show that a major section of your presentation has ended and a new one is beginning, pause, turn your back to the audience, and walk upstage. Then turn back, without pirouetting, to face front again. Don't speak while the audience is looking at your back! This is a dramatic, theatrical move. Know that whatever you say when you face the audience again will be seen as critical, so don't overuse this technique. It should be reserved for an important moment and used only *once* during a presentation or speech.

I spoke with one of our clients a few months after a workshop and asked him if he had incorporated any of the movement techniques we'd taught him. He laughed and said rather than using them in a business presentation, his most effective application came when arguing with his wife. I was surprised and asked him to give me the story. "Well, I know I can't play this card very often," he said, "but for dramatic emphasis, in the middle of an argument, I stopped, turned my back, and

> Turn your back on your audience only once during a speech.

took a few steps away from her. Then I turned around, faced her again, made my most important point—and she got it!"

Other Venues

When your space is confined, you still have options. With a podium, move from behind it, lean on it, or cross to the other side of it. Vary your physical relationship to display ease and control. Your only limitation will be the range of the microphone, if it's fixed.

If you are seated at a conference table, turn on an angle to make an important point. Sit up and lean forward slightly to indicate alertness and attention. Be careful of any tendency to slouch and form a C curve with your body. Keep your chest open to demonstrate your approachability and confidence. Turn to face the speaker next to you to show respect and consideration. Keep using your body to support your words. Show that you can master a space, however large or small.

With a handheld or wireless microphone, move away from the podium and practice "owning the room." Walk back to the podium only when you need to refer to your notes, take a drink of water, buy time to collect your thoughts, or advance your laptop to the next PowerPoint slide.

Spatial Accommodation

In a larger venue, you must occupy more space with movement and gestures, but that doesn't mean you have to ramp up your speaking style dramatically to match the boldness of the larger movements. Instead, keep your style warm, intimate, and direct, however large your stage. Actors call this "underplaying," and it can often be quite effective. Dial up the certainty and commitment, dial down the volume, and see how dynamic underplaying can be.

Speaking with a Microphone

If you are going to use a handheld microphone, rehearse with a small water bottle. Keep it about three inches away from and pointed at your chin. Leave the dramatic technique of holding the microphone directly in front of your mouth for contestants on "American Idol." For speakers, aiming a microphone at your mouth and getting too close to it can create distortion and unpleasant noises.

Practice angling your body to the left and right, while maintaining the same distance and relationship with the microphone. Dressing the cable (if it is not wireless) is important, so you don't trip on it: hold the cable in your opposite hand and clear it from your path with a flick of the wrist. Change hands to gesture. Practice until talking into the mike is second nature and becomes invisible to your audience.

If you have a lavalier microphone clipped to your clothing, rehearse turning your entire body as you move; otherwise, you will go "off mike" and lose volume when you turn your head away from it.

Practice with a microphone.

Moving with PowerPoint

PowerPoint poses its own specific challenges. A brightly lit screen with images, characters, and text will inevitably attract the eye more than a speaker. You must use movement to direct the audience's attention and maintain control. If *you* focus on the screen, so will the audience.

As you prepare your presentation and your slides, determine where you want the audience to look. If the space allows, stand on the same plane or next to the PowerPoint screen. If it is a large space, do not stand more than a foot or two downstage of the screen. That way, you can angle your body slightly toward the screen (as if it were a copresenter), which enables you to easily see and reference the slides without a change in body position. If you are so far downstage that you have to turn your back to look at the screen, your audience will follow your cue and look with you.

Don't fight a new PowerPoint slide. Give your audience a couple of seconds to absorb the content on the screen. When you want to regain focus and direct listeners' attention back to you, make a definitive move or hand gesture. Raise your voice. Walk toward the audience. Take off or put on your glasses. Pick up a prop. We're mammals and can't help but look when something moves.

If possible, stand in close proximity to the screen where your PowerPoint slides are projected.

These techniques will let the audience know *you* are directing the technical elements and not the other way around. It is your job to compel and persuade. Your visual elements are there to support you and add impact.

If you are advancing a PowerPoint program from your laptop yourself, practice using a remote. Simulate the conditions under which you will be presenting. Learn to work like a magician who gestures with one hand as a distraction while using the other to advance their slides.

Most of all, if you trip or lose your place, the computer breaks down, or the lights go off, learn to adapt. Presenters with poise use self-effacing humor to make a joke out of it and then continue. Remember the actor's motto "The show must go on." Laugh off a mistake of any magnitude, get back into your rhythm, and you will have a relieved, appreciative audience. It

Remember, the show must go on.

also shows you work well under pressure and can think on your feet.

Natural Is Best

At the beginning of this chapter, I said the goal is to use natural movement during your presentations. However, just because you move instinctively doesn't mean you will be effective.

Nathan is a large and imposing man, over six foot four with a big, booming voice. He speaks for a living as a business consultant and trainer. His natural tendency is to walk right up into the audience's collective face when he tells a story. This particular movement is intimidating and makes the audience back away. Humans have social contracts regarding space. Nathan didn't want to give up his habit of moving closer, so we persuaded him to lower his voice, which offset the feeling of physical intimidation. We kept his natural movement but adapted it to increase its effectiveness.

James, another Eloqui client, had a habit of rolling his shoulders back during his talk. Although he was very articulate and well versed in his topic, his shoulder rolling seemed at odds with his expertise and soon became distracting. Our attention is easily captured by people's physical mannerisms, and they pull focus away from content when they are not in harmony with the rest of the presentation.

As I listened carefully, I noticed that James's shoulder rolls only occurred when he spoke about his job as a mortgage broker. After interviewing him, I learned that he was uncomfortable in his present career and would rather be doing something else. The shoulder roll was his unconscious way of trying to make his suit—and metaphorically, his job—fit better. As James saw the relationship, he eliminated this distracting habit, and not surprisingly, he also changed jobs.

THE GOLDEN RULE

Use whatever movement is natural and true for you. Just as your presentation should sound conversational and as close to your personal style as possible, your movements should reflect your normal behavior. Try out the various moves described in this chapter. Take the ones that seem effective for you and rehearse them until they begin to feel like yours. Remember, practice makes natural. Shakespeare had Hamlet advise a local troupe of actors not to ham it up so they would be believable. Hamlet said, "Suit the action to the word, the word to the action; with this special observance, that you overstep not the modesty of nature." Although written in the late 1500s, this is still great advice.

9

PowerPoint Revival

Imagine being a juror at a trial and being forced to sit through closing arguments that take two and a half hours and include 253 PowerPoint slides! Is your first thought utter dread? As a captive audience, you have nowhere to hide, no Blackberry or cell phone to check, and you will soon be asked to render a critical decision based on what you have seen and heard. Like a wolf caught in a trap, do you feel like chewing off your leg as a viable option for escape?

These were the circumstances in a high-stakes trial, where the pharmaceutical company Merck was sued by the widow of a man who died after taking the company's drug Vioxx. Yet surprisingly, the jury saw a PowerPoint presentation so riveting and so powerful that it was labeled CSI: PowerPoint, and the plaintiff's family was awarded $253 million—or $1million per slide. Cliff Atkinson, journalist, MBA, and author of *Beyond Bullet Points*, designed the winning presentation. He constructed and organized the 253 slides into a three-act play and, like any good story, included compelling characters, strong conflict, resolution, and most of all, *visuals*.

Atkinson and other authorities like Edward Tufte, a Yale professor and design expert, are doing their best to move the business world away from the narcoleptic effect of standardized PowerPoint presentations that are nothing more than cuing devices for the presenter. "PowerPoint doesn't give presentations; PowerPoint makes slides," says Matt Thornhill, president of Audience First. "Remember that you are creating slides to support a spoken presentation." But, pressed for time and lacking creativity, too many business professionals create heavily text-rich slides, and little is differentiated or compelling. Instead of engaging the audience, their goal is to ensure that nothing is left out. Visuals take a backseat or are nonexistent. Content leads and, in the process, saps every bit of personality and vitality out of the presenter.

> PowerPoint doesn't give presentations; it creates slides. *You* give the presentation.

We know from cognitive science that the brain processes information in dual channels—visual and verbal. PowerPoint is the visual channel, and speaking is the verbal channel. People learn best when the spoken word and pictures are presented together. However, the words and visuals need to complement one other and make connections between the information presented and what we already know. Otherwise, because of limited capacity, when our brains are overloaded, we will ignore one or the other.

Using PowerPoint the way Cliff Atkinson did for the Merck trial—employing emotional visuals, and building pacing and momentum like any good narrative—is rare in business today. For those who are willing to break the rules, PowerPoint doesn't have to be tedious. It is a widely available, highly malleable, and creative tool for any business professional.

> PowerPoint doesn't have to be tedious!

A BETTER WAY

Dean is the CEO of a company that distributes quality branded products to cabinetmakers and architectural millwork shops. After his company was acquired by a German conglomerate, he was asked to attend a conference in Germany and speak on turning a profit during tough economic times. Dean contracted with Eloqui because he wanted to deliver a convincing talk that positioned his newly acquired company as a leader in their industry. Initially, Dean was going to lead off with a PowerPoint presentation that went straight to the point and detailed the actual numbers. David and Deborah encouraged him to come up with an opening analogy to better frame his argument and be more persuasive, especially to an audience for whom English was a second language. They then recommended that his PowerPoint support this frame to give it added credence and power. Dean left the session and totally revised his presentation.

With his first slide of a photograph of a private airplane, he began this way:

> Two and a half years ago, I made a decision to become a pilot. One of the first lessons in my training was the importance of a good instrument scan and the function of control and performance instruments. This is similar to what each of us does every day in managing our business. The instrument scan is like looking over the cockpit—graphs that show how we are performing in our companies.
>
> Sales are like the airspeed indicator, telling us how fast we are moving, and growth is like the altimeter indicating a climb or a descent. These are just two of the performance instruments that show the results of how I'm flying the plane. And then there is the control instrument that displays a change in direction. Gross profit is a control instrument that indicates the direction of a company. When action is taken to improve gross profit,

overall performance of the company improves right to the bottom line—the operating income. This morning I'll give you a couple of techniques we acted on at our company to improve gross profit in 2008.

As Dean spoke about each of the instrument panels, a photo was superimposed over the graphs and charts of his company's yearly numbers. The audience could easily make the association of instrument flying with company financials, and Dean kept his listeners engaged. His slides supported his content, and he was the lead, piloting his presentation to where he wanted to take his audience.

There is a simple axiom Eloqui tells their clients: "As a speaker, you are the interpreter presenting in partnership with Power-Point." Dean had a passion for flying and found an exciting way to link specific visuals out of the audience's knowledge base to the

Two Versions

If minimizing the content or reducing your slide count is simply not possible, consider constructing two PowerPoint presentations. The leaner, more graphic version is the one that is projected. As the narrator, you fill in the details that are not on the screen. The more detailed, text-rich version is the one you give your audience or client as a handout at the conclusion of your talk. Just be sure to alert the audience near the beginning of your presentation that you will pass out a more detailed version after you conclude. You don't want audience members or clients frustrated because they think they need to remember the more detailed information presented in your PowerPoint. Knowing they will receive a text-rich copy at the end mitigates this concern.

financial data he delivered. Treat the information on each slide as if it was coded in a foreign language and the audience needs you to make sense of or interpret it.

THE PSYCHOLOGY OF EFFECTIVE POWERPOINT

There are two ways that information is embedded into working memory: auditory and visual. Each can support or compete with one another. Understanding how we process information forms the basis for effective PowerPoint. To use PowerPoint optimally, show a graphic on the screen as you talk about it. Because our brain's processing capacity is limited, we can combine information coming in through both our eyes and ears, but only if they work together.

> What you say and what you show on PowerPoint must not compete with each other.

Whether I'm working with graduate students or corporate presenters, there is the same look of anguish when I encourage them to remove text from their slides. I have to pry each bullet point from the screen. Then, as they try out their graphics-based approach and see the difference in their audience's response, it's like a religious conversion. The feedback they receive makes them want to know about video editing software, sites for copyright-free graphics (two good clip art sites include http://pro.corbis.com and http://hemera.com), and graphics editing software. These are the real tools of PowerPoint. The essence of a slide should be what you can say better with a visual than you can with words.

> The essence of every PowerPoint slide should be visual.

As Cliff Atkinson recommends, use PowerPoint like a movie or play. Craft titles that tease the content of the slide. Drive the overall presentation to a climax and resolution. The goal is to have your audience engaged and remember your content.

THE ADVANCEMENT OF POWERPOINT

PowerPoint was developed to work around the problems of slides and transparencies, which took many days to create and then could not be edited easily. With PowerPoint, technology geeks could create last-minute slides electronically without design support and for almost no cost. The program created a popular new trend. Supposedly, you did not need the skills, talent, or experience of professional designers, if you had access to their tools. It was like saying that if you were given a set of oil paints and brushes, you would be able to produce works in the same league as Renoir, Raphael, and Picasso. If this example seems absurd, you begin to understand the problems brought on by PowerPoint.

After the people at Microsoft had seen enough poorly conceived electronic slides, they thought they would solve the problem by creating PowerPoint templates called wizards. The wizards provided stock graphics and backgrounds that unfortunately ensured that every slide would look the same. Microsoft also developed wizards that outlined the order and structured the text on each slide. This drove business professionals to construct nearly identical PowerPoint presentations. A sample template screen from a PowerPoint wizard is shown on the facing page.

Although the wizards served as a prompt for speakers who were unclear about what to include or omit, it soon seemed that every PowerPoint presentation had its big headline and three to six bullet items per screen. The software became the Brooks Brothers suit of presentations. It stripped out individuality, creativity, and self-expression. The wizards led to the antithesis of effective, successful presentations. The results were so consistently dull that the wizard designers would no longer allow vendors pitching business to use PowerPoint in their presentations.

SAMPLE OF POWERPOINT WIZARD

Ideas for Today and Tomorrow

Vision Statement
- State the vision and long-term direction

Goal and Objective
- State the desired goal
- State the desired objective
- Use multiple points if necessary

Today's Situation
- Summary of the current situation
- Use brief bullets, discuss details verbally

How Did We Get Here?
- Any relevant historical information
- Original assumptions that are no longer valid

Available Options
- State the alternative strategies
- List advantages and disadvantages of each
- State cost of each option

Recommendation
- Recommend one or more of the strategies
- Summarize the results if things go as proposed
- What to do next
- Identify action items

CREATING COUNTERPOINT

When you listen to the music of Johann Sebastian Bach, you hear one of the greatest examples of counterpoint. It is a musical technique in which two or more melodies are played at the same time. Although each melody is beautiful by itself, they intertwine. They support and lift each other, creating a whole far greater than the sum of its parts. At any moment in time, the notes from the different melodies are in harmony with each other.

In much the same way, when you deliver a presentation with PowerPoint, the slides are also making a presentation. If you work together with that presentation, beautiful counterpoint is produced, and each improves the other. If you compete, the result is distraction and disharmony. When you use PowerPoint, your presentation's success depends on the relationship you create between what you say and what you have on the screen. Your job as the presenter is to look at the overall relationship between the two and make sure they support each other.

The Gettysburg Address as PowerPoint

Examine the slides shown on the next page, which present the Gettysburg Address as a PowerPoint presentation. They were developed by Peter Norvig using a wizard. How do you think this version compares to the original?

This presentation is not an improvement on Lincoln's speech. Some of the main elements are included, but it lacks any emotional appeal, poetry, or persuasion. The question now becomes, "How can you overcome the curse of the wizard?"

AVOIDING PITFALLS

PowerPoint gives you the potential to create extraordinary presentations, but also gives you the potential to make your presenta-

GETTYSBURG CEMETERY DEDICATION
Abraham Lincoln

Agenda
- Met on battlefield (great)
- Dedicate portion of field—fitting!
- Unfinished work (great tasks)

Not on Agenda!
- Dedicate
- Consecrate
- Hallow (in narrow sense)
- Add or detract
- Note or remember what
  we say

Review of Key Objectives and Critical Success Factors
- What makes nation unique
  - Conceived in Liberty
  - Men are equal
- Shared vision
  - New birth of freedom
  - Gov't of/for/by the people

Organizational Overview

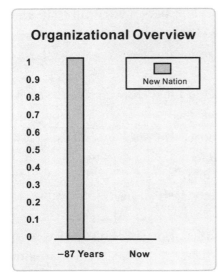

Summary
- New nation
- Civil war
- Dedicate field
- Dedicated to unfinished
  work
- New birth of freedom
- Government not perish

tions boring and utterly forgettable. Because PowerPoint already has such a bad reputation, there are ways to accentuate the positive and avoid the negative.

Words Versus Visuals

As the speaker, you are better at using words than PowerPoint is. You can put more emotion into the text; physically move to support your content; emphasize or deemphasize various phrases; and vary your volume, pitch, and tempo.

An experienced musician can pick up a music score and read the notes. He imagines what the music will sound like, but it rarely moves him as much as actually hearing the music played. Music was around long before people learned to write it down as musical notation. Sheet music is very useful for communicating what notes to play, and there are symbols to suggest how expressively to play the notes, but it's *not* music. Spoken language was around for centuries before it was recorded. Having an audience read three bullet points is rarely a substitute for hearing the emotion and personality you put into speaking about them. Worse still is that your listeners will be reading the bullet points along with you—and they read a lot faster than you speak.

> You are better at using words than PowerPoint is.

It's also a pain to read a great deal of text from a screen, and by the time the audience or client has read and absorbed a lengthy passage, they have lost what you just said. Try an experiment. Pick up a newspaper, look at a headline, and try *not* to read it. It is nearly impossible. At this point in your life, your reading skills are automatic. If text is placed in front of you, you will read it. If audience members are listening to you speak, and at the same time, you project a screen covered in

> Direct the audience's attention to one key message per slide.

text, they will read it and not listen to you, just as you read the headline while trying not to. This means you have moved their attention away from your talk and redirected it to the screen. Why would you want to compete with a screen, especially when it will win?

Better to use graphics, photos, animation, or other visuals to snapshot your content and then speak to it. PowerPoint lets you do just that. How effective is it to use words to describe the sound of a violin, the way to hit a tennis ball, or the look of next year's hybrid SUV? There is a growing trend among professionals to use PowerPoint only for graphics.

Building a Deck

Reduce the number of slides to as few as possible and direct your audience's attention to one key takeaway, or message, per slide.

Gone with the Wind

The problem with constructing text-rich slides often begins with the titles. For more than seven years, Deborah was brought into Amgen to work with executives and medical professionals on their presentations and supporting PowerPoint decks. Consistently, the individual slides had titles that were as many as three lines long. Lengthy titles *and* text guarantee the audience will split their focus; words on the screen will dominate, and the audience will pay less attention to the speaker. The problem was that every Amgen slide had to go through "pink folder" checking for compliance by their legal department. Deborah recommended the presenters tease the content of the slide with the title—and eliminate any reference to medical information that would red flag the attorneys.

Believing that the title needs to include a summary of everything to be covered in the slide creates a giant

Use short, catchy titles on your PowerPoint slides.

hurdle. You want your audience to scan the data on the screen and return to you for clarification and examples, as soon as possible. Eloqui recommends having fun with the titles, and keeping them short, punchy and clever.

Nuke the Sub-Bullets

Rather than diluting important information and writing out entire sentences, construct key points as bullets. And whenever possible, eliminate the sub-points. These secondary bullets are typically reminders to the presenter of what to cover. But if you know your content, they are unnecessary and create visual clutter. Rehearse or practice how you will interpret the bullets for your audience, relating examples and metaphors or expanding on the phrases. Question how the information relates to the audience's experience. Create an association, such as how the data relates to client service. Delivered this way, the audience or client can scan the information on the screen and quickly return to you, the presenter, for the application or how best to interpret it.

PowerPoint should emphasize these main points and facilitate organization. Sometimes your hands are tied because of regulatory requirements or your company's legal department, or you are given a PowerPoint deck with long sections of text and told to leave it exactly as is. There are things you can do to encourage scanning and quickly drive the attention back to you, even with screens packed with text. The simplest way to emphasize key points is to boldface, underline, or highlight key phrases. Use a different color font. Direct your listeners' attention to the content *you* want them to focus on. And if even these devices are rejected or not available to you, make the content your own by giving verbal examples to feature or bring to life what is on the screen.

Font Size

When it comes to screen type, size matters. Whenever possible, visit the room in which you will be presenting. If you can't, ask for the room's dimensions, the seating arrangements, and the location of the screen. People quickly get frustrated when they try to read text that is too small.

A conservative rule for the amount of text on a screen is "6 × 6," or no more than six lines on a screen and no more than six words per line. Do not treat this rule as gospel. To be safe in determining appropriate text from various distances, use the following guidelines: for every ten feet from the screen, add a half inch (36 points) to your font size.

- If the distance is ten feet, use 36-point type.
- If the distance is twenty feet, use 72-point type.
- If the distance is thirty feet, use 108-point type.
- If the distance is forty feet, use 144-point type.
- If the distance is fifty feet, use 180-point type.

This formula guarantees that everyone will be able to read your slides easily from anywhere in the room.

The Best Use of PowerPoint

The true power of PowerPoint is its ability to create relationships between objects, concepts, or ideas. The program allows you to place text in boxes, triangles, or circles and use arrows to show how they connect. To show dominance, you can give these shapes various sizes and or move them with simple animation. Be creative in how you construct your PowerPoint slides, and you will keep your client or audience engaged.

Be careful of using PowerPoint to introduce new information. When you have to deliver a sizable amount of content, especially if it is technically complex or difficult to grasp, and the audience hasn't seen it before, use concrete language, create associations to what your audience already knows, and give examples that bring the technical information to life. Although PowerPoint has the capacity to present any information, it is your job to keep the momentum and pacing moving forward and not get bogged down in any one particular section.

Don't Read Your Slides—Ever

Reading slides to your audience is the single most annoying, ineffective, and damaging abuse of PowerPoint. Reading titles, bullet points, or paragraphs of text is offensive and patronizing. Reading is such a well-practiced habit that you barely have control over doing it. That's why companies spend so much money on print ads. They know you will read them because they are there.

The average college-educated adult reads approximately 250 words per minute. That same reader's average speech rate is approximately 125 words per minute. If you read the six bullet points on your PowerPoint slide, by the time you have completed number three, audience members have already finished reading number six. Then they wait for you. Limit your text to a bare minimum, then consider how you can edit even more of it out.

Graphics and Slide Design

When you import graphics, make sure they are of the highest quality. Don't enlarge a bitmapped image that will pixilate. It is a poor, bitmapped image that has been enlarged and is now pixilated.

Poor, low-resolution graphics tell your audience you have low standards and don't pay attention to detail.

It shows your audience that you are not very discriminating and have low standards and expectations. It also shows a lack of attention to detail. In most cases, the PowerPoint wizards keep you from creating unprofessional slides, although you can still override them and produce visual cacophony. If you are not an experienced graphic designer or don't know one, then it is acceptable to use PowerPoint's visual designs.

Directing Focus

Artistic presentations are wonderful, and graphic color combinations can be dazzling, but in PowerPoint you need to provide enough contrast between the text and backgrounds. Remember, clarity *before* art. Make sure the text contrasts well with the background. The smaller the text, the more important this principle becomes.

> Be economical with what you emphasize on your PowerPoint slides.

One problem presenters often have is their belief that most of what they say is important, so they must emphasize that text. They do it by using italics, boldface, underlining, different colored text, and various fonts. Remember this Zen paradox: if you emphasize everything, you emphasize nothing. Save your emphasis for the few times when it is essential. Another useful guideline from the print world is that italics *whisper* and boldface **screams**.

Avoid placing keywords in different fonts or even mixing different fonts at all. Use one font (at most two) all the way through: one serif font (one with little lines on the letters, as with Times) and one sans serif font (one with plain, unornamented letters, like Arial). If you prefer, choose one style for headers and the other for supporting text.

> Use one or, at most, two fonts on your PowerPoint slides.

White Space

Because most of us have grown up with print in books, magazines, newspapers, and journals, we are used to seeing massive amounts of crowded text. This makes sense when every additional page increases the amount of paper, storage, and shipping. In contrast, PowerPoint needs space around the text to be easily absorbed and the attention returned to the presenter. With PowerPoint, if you have three bullet points, you can place them together on one slide, build them one at a time and then screen them back (i.e., making the last point fade into the background before the new point appears), or you can feature each point on its own slide. When something is set off with space around it, your eye is drawn to it.

Transitions

One of the features PowerPoint gives you is a set of transitions to take you from slide to slide, including dissolving, wiping, and appearing from the center out. Find *one* that you like and use it throughout your presentation. Make it as unobtrusive as possible so it will not be distracting. If you have distinct sections within your presentation, use a specific transition to indicate each one. Too often, people get seduced

> Find one transition style you like and stick with it!

Next . . .

The best way to use transitions is to make them functional. For example, if you use a book graphic, use a right-to-left wipe to give the appearance of a page turning. If you use a notepad background, you can use a bottom-to-top wipe for the same effect. If you transition from one graph to another, place the axes at the same location on each slide, and you can use a dissolve to give the illusion of animation. This works for any related graphics where you want to show contrast.

by the dazzling technology of transitions and use as many as they can. What exacerbates the problem is that you can buy additional third-party transitions that are wilder and more distracting than the ones Microsoft gives you. Resist the temptation.

Building Blocks

The strategy of putting a great deal of information on one slide and playing *Where's Waldo?* to find what's important makes little sense. There are a number of techniques to direct the audience's focus to each section of essential content. You can list key points. You can build your list, adding items each time you click on your remote or laptop. You can take one section at a time and enlarge it to fill the center of your slide; once you have finished talking about this particular section, you can then "screen it back" so that it blends with the background, as mentioned previously. The audience will focus on whichever point is front and center. You can also separate information onto separate slides unless all of the information must be seen together to improve comprehension.

Sound Off?

If you have a sound that complements your presentation, such as quotes, client testimonials, or the specific sound of your product, use it. However, if you are considering playing music underneath your entire presentation, or during the transitions, key points or when your logo appears full screen, weigh this idea very carefully. Sounds can be distracting and keep your audience from absorbing your message. Remember that the brain cannot perform two difficult tasks at the same time. If your listeners are listening to the music, it takes their full attention away from you and your message.

Use music sparingly.

To B or Not to B

The *B* and *W* keys are well-kept PowerPoint secrets but essential for presenters. If you press the *B* key, your screen will go black or blue until you hit another key. If you hit the *W* key, the screen goes white. (Note: Black is preferable because it lets you be seen and does not have the glare of a white screen.) During the time the screen is blank, you do not have to compete with it. You have the audience's entire attention and can tell an anecdote, cross downstage, move in front of the screen, or do the unexpected. When you hit the same button again, the current slide reappears.

> The B and W keys are underused PowerPoint tools—so use them!

Some handheld-remote vendors, including Logitech, now include the *B* key on their products. If your remote does not have this feature, build in a black screen at the appropriate time(s) to grab your listeners' focus.

HANDOUTS

The following recommendations concerning handouts—whether they are PowerPoint slides, the whole deck, or collateral material— are derived from our collective experience. Our objective is that the focus always be on the presenter and our knowledge that when you give audience members or clients something to read and process, they will.

Double-Edged Sword

I once taught a class in a lab where every student was seated in front of a computer with an Internet connection. Keeping the students' attention was a monumental task because whenever I stopped engaging them, I saw their eyes lower from me to anything_enter taining.com. As a presenter, if you put something in an audience member's hands during your presentation, the temptation to read it is like trying to resist the apple in the Garden of Eden. You are guaranteeing a distraction from your presentation. The handout will draw focus away from you.

Just because you have a lot to say doesn't mean you have to say it all with your PowerPoint slides. Narrow your focus, but present each supporting point in a way that is so clear, fascinating, and thought-provoking that the audience will be riveted. Then, at the end of your presentation, distribute a handout to read at their leisure; you have not distracted them during your talk.

Let your audience know up front that, at the conclusion of your talk, you will be giving them a handout; tell them what it contains. This will satisfy their desire to capture and retain all of your engaging material and allow them to put their full attention on you.

Now Is Good

There are times when handouts are valuable *during* your presentation. To prevent them from becoming a distraction, make sure they contain only supporting materials that make little sense without your explanation. Certain corporations or organizations insist on receiving handouts during a presentation because attendees need to take notes for professional credit, or the handout provides additional information that needs to be used during a break-out session, a quiz, or an evaluation that must be filled out and turned in.

Here are a few conditions that necessitate using handouts during your presentation:

▪ **Structured interactive exercises:** There are times when you will engage your audience in an interactive activity, either one-on-one or in a breakout session in small groups. If the participants need certain materials, the handout is instructive. Such handouts may contain a template for the exercise, a set of vignettes or case studies to discuss, and so on. Make it clear that the handout will only make sense in context and that you will alert the participants when and how to use it.

■ **Technical vocabulary and diagrams:** There are times when you may need to use some specialized terms that are difficult to write and pronounce. In most cases, it would be better for you to present them in the body of a PowerPoint presentation, but there are times when it is more efficient for the audience to have these references in front of them. Audience members may wish to enter their own comments or additions on the handouts.

■ **Foreign audience members:** If you are presenting technical information to people whose first language is not English, it may be helpful to have certain terms written out. Your audience may be used to reading the terms but unfamiliar with hearing them, and a visual reference is useful.

Proceed at Your Own Risk

Whenever you use handouts, pay as much attention to preparing them as you do to preparing your presentation. If you have typos, poor grammar, low-resolution graphics, or clumsy assembly of various parts, you will leave a negative impression. If you have some skill with desktop publishing software such as InDesign, Quark, or Pagemaker, use it. Make the information attractive, useful, and engaging. Your handouts are an extension of your presentation. They represent you.

Handouts are not limited to paper. Consider putting them on CDs, DVDs, or a website so that you can use video, animation, graphics, and sound. Be careful not to substitute glitz for substance. They still must be helpful in achieving your intention.

MECHANICS OF DELIVERY

The most intelligent and well-crafted PowerPoint cannot present itself. Consider the PowerPoint as your partner. There needs to be a balance between the two of you. To be most effective, pay attention to the way you hand off to the screen, feature the visual content, and create counterpoint so that the PowerPoint never dominates.

The Boy Scout Motto

Always check your equipment and rehearse on-site. If you bring your own laptop to use with someone else's projector, make sure they are compatible and work together seamlessly. Today, there are a huge variety of presentation devices. Some presenters will travel with just a flash drive, CD-ROM, or DVD, confident that they can use it with any computer. But if you formatted your CD-ROM on a Mac, it may not work on the version of Windows you will be using. Many PDA devices let you store and run PowerPoint. Check the compatibility with available equipment well in advance of your presentation. Always have a backup plan.

Breakdown

I was at a large government conference, attending a PowerPoint presentation, when the screen when blank. As the presenter began checking the connections from his computer to the LCD projector, a man came running in to stop him. He wore a large button identifying him as a member of the projectionists' union and claimed that only he was allowed to work on the equipment. Within a minute or two, it became clear to the speaker and everyone else on the platform that this union man was inexperienced with any technology newer than a 16-mm film projector, but that didn't stop him from keeping everyone else away.

It took fifteen minutes before someone got the idea to ask the union projectionist for a pair of long-nosed pliers. While he was gone, the speaker fixed the problem in less than a minute, and when the union man returned, they told him, "It just started working again." But what would have happened to the presentation if the projector bulb had burned out and there was no replacement bulb? Or if the computer had gone down or the Internet connection had stopped working?

Eloqui has hundreds of client stories of setbacks, stalls, breakdowns, and technological failures surrounding the use of Power-Point. Whenever technology is involved, the possibility of error is magnified. As a speaker, you *must* be ready to make your presentation without PowerPoint. Not only will the audience give you extra marks for stepping out in front of the technology, but you will demonstrate expertise in your field and your ability to creatively overcome tough problems on the spot.

> You must be prepared to make your presentation without PowerPoint.

Know the Material

Review your PowerPoint presentation until you are very familiar with the order of the slides. If you keep looking over your shoulder or at your laptop to see what is on the screen, you will distract your audience. Furthermore, there may be times when you want to advance quickly through your presentation or go back to a previous slide to highlight a different graphic or respond to a question. Knowing your slide order demonstrates your competence and thorough preparation.

Interacting with the Big Screen

Blocking, as we discussed in Chapter 8, is the term film and stage directors use when positioning actors. It is also an essential component for PowerPoint presenters. Rather than positioning yourself midway between the big screen and the audience, stand or sit as close to the screen as possible. You don't want your audience visually "ping-ponging" back and forth between you and the screen.

When you stand next to the screen, you can gesture at an important item, graph, or chart to better emphasize your point. This is not always possible, especially if there are two screens on either side of you or you need to be close to your laptop to advance the slides. In these instances, maintain as much eye contact as possible with your audience and minimize the number of times you turn back to gesture or look at the screen or your laptop.

Years ago, Eloqui was training engineers in Silicon Valley who consistently worked with PowerPoint. Shy by nature, they would inevitably face the screen rather than make eye contact with the audience. Deborah reminded them to comb the back of their hair, because that was primarily what the audience saw. (Even engineers have a sense of humor.) Laser pointers can highlight items on the screen and maintain flexibility for positioning. However, some clients have expressed irritation over the jerky motion of the laser's red light. Be careful not to overuse the laser pointer and give your audience a headache.

When you position yourself next to the screen, keep your chest open to the audience rather than standing in profile. Facing the screen at a forty-five-degree angle gives the impression that you are in partnership with PowerPoint. Conversely, if you face the audience directly and do not turn slightly toward the screen, the impression is that you are separate from your visual presentation.

> When you face the screen, do so at a forty-five-degree angle.

Take Back Control

During a typical Eloqui training, the trainers place the section on PowerPoint near the end of the session. They want to be sure the participants know how to effectively structure their content, keep an audience engaged, and construct various safety nets to allow them to think quickly on their feet. Yet even with this extensive preparation, the Eloqui trainers can accurately predict that the section on PowerPoint will adversely affect participants' presentation skills. What is it about PowerPoint that kicks people back to the default mode of stiff, boring, and forgettable presenting?

Eloqui believes that business professionals are trained to focus primarily on content, with little regard for engaging the audience or delivering the material. Add PowerPoint to the mix and it becomes too easy to read the slides; relate material in a linear, chronological fashion; and use the technology as a cuing device rather than a colorful partner. This is called the default mode.

Changing this paradigm takes commitment and practice. Once you know your content, what matters most is how you deliver it so that it grabs the audience's attention and achieves your objective. With PowerPoint, avoid the trap of predictability and letting the audience get ahead of you. Watch the next PowerPoint presenter for the way she interacts with slides. Invariably, she will advance the slide, speak to it, and then click to the next slide. Slide, speak, click. Slide, speak, click. After just a few slides, the audience or client has already figured out the pattern and is most likely bored.

Break the pattern. Advance the slide *before* you've finished speaking about the content on the prior slide. Or speak to the next slide and *then* advance it. Make the screen blank (or black) to tell an anecdote or cross in front of it. When a list comes up on a slide, don't start at the beginning and work your way down. Start in the middle of the list. Or tell the audience that everything is valuable, but you want to draw attention to item number five because . . . If you don't follow a prescribed pattern, the audience has to pay attention to you or lose the thread of your presentation.

> Don't fall into a prescribed pattern when advancing your slides.

You also control the audience's attention through physical movement and gestures. Eloqui recommends starting and ending your presentations standing still; this is when the audience is reading all the signals about who you are and what the presentation is about. However, once the presentation is under way, there is no good reason (unless the microphone is fixed to the podium) to stand in one spot.

When you want your listeners to focus on you, turn to face them and talk. Include a move downstage. If you are sharing an aside or insight, move directly toward the audience. If you are making an important point, cross downstage, even if it means moving in front of the screen. End your move outside of the projected light. And when you want the audience to refocus on a PowerPoint slide, turn your body toward the screen, which signals that you want others to do the same.

When a new slide appears, there are a couple of options for regaining the attention of your listeners. First, give them a few seconds to absorb the content or scan the slide. Then raise your voice (singers call it "attack") or move. Whether it's taking off your glasses, picking up a prop, or physically changing locations, the audience's eyes will follow the movement. And remember, you can always hit the *B* and *W* keys to regain focus and leave nothing to distract the audience from your presentation.

PUTTING IT ALL IN PERSPECTIVE

You are the star. PowerPoint is your backup and support system. Every performance can be successful. First, determine your intention or objective. What is it you most want to achieve or have the audience do? If your objective is only to educate or inform, we predict your PowerPoint presentation will include too much data and you will most likely ramble or

> You are the star; PowerPoint is your backup and support system.

deliver more information than is necessary or relevant. However, if your objective is to persuade or motivate your audience to take action, your PowerPoint presentation can be an influential partner and attention grabber.

Once you have determined your objective, construct your slides to bolster and achieve this outcome. Devise a theme to revisit throughout the presentation. Look for visuals to illuminate key points; show the relationship between statistics and results; and demonstrate contrast, progression, or context rather than reading items from a list. With bullet points, present them out of order so your audience turns to you for clarification and insight. Then rehearse the presentation along with your slides. Include everything from where to aim the remote and the location of your laptop to how quickly to advance the slides. Knowing your content is only a small fraction of the necessary preparation to ensure success.

Think of this chapter as a checklist to help you avoid falling into the PowerPoint Bermuda Triangle. When you are successful with PowerPoint, you will be memorable, persuasive, and effective. As you prepare, keep asking yourself this key question: "Can I do a better job saying it or showing it?" Every time you answer, "Showing it," think PowerPoint. When the answer is "Saying it," focus your attention on vivid ways to verbally convey your ideas *without* PowerPoint.

Think of yourself as a director making a movie and deciding on the best way to display the meaning and emotion you want to convey. Visual media can be enormously powerful. Just as stories, examples, and anecdotes are memorable, your use of media and images will add to the complete impact and integrity of your presentation. Go for the most persuasive graphics you can find. Use stunning, unique images; convincing graphs; and attention-sustaining animation and video. Or hire a graphic designer who specializes in Power-Point presentations.

> Ask yourself, "Can I do a better job saying it or showing it?"

OTHER TECHNOLOGIES

So far, we have only talked about PowerPoint, but there are many other software packages that apply the same principles as well as new technologies.

Smartboards

Smartboards have replaced chalkboards and have many advantages, besides the fact that they do not generate chalk dust. These boards use special markers in many colors and can be wiped clean with tissue or paper towels. Their real advantage, however, is that the content of the boards may be saved on a computer and also printed out and distributed.

Figure out who should do the writing or drawing. If you are creating graphics and drawing diagrams that clarify your presentation information, you should obviously wield the marker. If you are recording input from the group in an interactive presentation, it's generally better to have someone else do the writing, so you can keep your attention on running the presentation and facilitating the interaction. Designate someone in advance rather than attempting to select a volunteer. This way, you can be assured that the person has the necessary skills and willingness to do the task.

Videoconferencing

A few years ago, I saw a funny Dilbert cartoon. Dilbert came home and told his dog that he had just spent five thousand dollars on an exotic videoconferencing system, then his dog asked him if he knew anyone else who had one. Today, videoconferencing costs much less as long as you have a broadband Internet connection. This technology saves travel expenses but requires a few new skill sets.

If you just want to sit in front of a small video camera and talk to one other person, then the biggest concern is whether your hair looks OK or what you should wear. Once you have multiple participants and data sharing, the task becomes more difficult. Most of the techniques in this chapter still apply if you are making a presentation in this way, but remember that you are now being seen by your audience in a small video window.

THE FINAL POINT

PowerPoint demands a marriage of art and science. Although the technology has advanced rapidly in the last few years, the tendency in most presentations is for the slide deck to be front and center, with the speaker fading into the background. We must reverse this equation, so the presenter is always the featured act, with Power-Point supporting, clarifying, and illustrating the content. A picture (or slide) can be worth a thousand words. Or so convoluted that it takes a thousand words to explain it.

10

Being Memorable

You have just made your last car payment and the bank sends you the pink slip. Of course, you want to store this important document in a safe place. If you are well organized, you may have a safety deposit box or a special desk drawer for such valuable papers. On the other hand, if you are not well organized, you search for and eventually find a secure place to store it. Unfortunately, like many of us, you may have trouble remembering the location of your new safe place. Think about how often you have agonized over forgetting where something was.

If you replace the pink slip with any piece of information and the physical location with your audience's memory, you now understand the challenge. In a presentation, it is the presenter who chooses that safe place. How you select your stories and anecdotes, organize your material, and make your presentation interactive determines how well your listeners remember what they hear. Plus, these same principles can be applied to how well *you* remember your own material.

Remember the last time you went to a great talk or lecture, one that had you riveted. You were enriched, informed, perhaps even transformed. Then, in your exuberance to share your newfound wisdom, you told a friend about it. You recalled it in as much detail as you could remember. If the original lecture lasted an hour, how long did it take you to repeat everything you could remember? Five or six minutes? What happened to the rest of the information?

Now think about what you remember from a talk that was only mediocre or boring, even if it was accompanied by PowerPoint slides. Not much of the content stuck. As a presenter, you must do three things to be persuasive and have people remember what you say:

- Grab and keep their attention.
- Make sure they understand what you say in a meaningful way.
- Organize your material so it will be remembered and easily retrieved.

To accomplish these goals, it is essential to understand a few basic concepts that explain how memory works.

LEARNING AND MEMORY

Memory is linked to learning. Obviously, your listeners cannot remember an important point from your presentation if they don't learn it first. Learning means acquiring new information. It can be finding out someone's name or figuring out how to use a program like PowerPoint. Memory is being able to remember that information after you have learned it.

Learning and memory have a critical relationship. The *way* you learn something determines how you will remember it. The key to making memory efficient is organization. If new information is well organized and relates to what you already know, it is easier to remember. For example, as a child, you probably spelled words using the letters *e*, *i*, and *c* correctly by learning a simple organizing principle: *i* before *e* except after *c*, or when sounded like *a* in *neighbor* or *weigh*. Many of us have relied on this rule throughout our adult lives.

Adding to Your Memory

Two psychologists, R. A. Sulin and D. J. Dooling, conducted a unique experiment to show how memories are changed on the spot, demonstrating that people aren't aware of how or where their information comes from. Furthermore, that we take in every new piece of information and change it by combining what we already know and believe. In this experiment, Sulin and Dooling had people read one of two passages. Read the following passage, cover it, and then answer the question that comes after it.

Need for Professional Help

Carol Harris was a problem child from birth. She was wild, stubborn, and violent. By the time Carol turned eight, she was unmanageable. Her parents were very concerned about her mental health. There was no good institution for her problem in the State. Her parents finally decided to take some action. They hired a private teacher for Carol.

Now cover up the passage without looking at it again and answer this question: Was the sentence "She was deaf and blind" contained in the passage you just read? Yes or no?

Most likely, you did not think that sentence was in the original passage. Would it surprise you to know that almost half of the people in the study said it was? They did, and here's why. The people who thought the sentence was there read a passage that was identical to the one you just read except for one big difference. The name Carol Harris was changed to Helen Keller. Most people reading the version with Helen Keller's name already knew that Helen Keller was deaf and blind, so when they heard that sentence, they added it to their memory of the passage—even though it was never mentioned. Because memory is active and not passive, they remembered what they knew about Helen Keller rather than whether or not the specific sentence was present. What we learn and remember is influenced by what we already have stored in our memories.

Memory Is Dynamic

Remembering is not like putting socks in a drawer and pulling them out later to have them look just the same as when you put them in. You cannot put something into your brain and pull it out later in the same form. Remembering is an active process. You change stored information as you learn it. This information continues to change as it combines with what you already know and as new information continues to come in. Put simply, your memory is constantly being revised and reconstructed.

The topic of memory is neglected or totally omitted from most presentation books. This is a major oversight because it gets at one of the most fundamental reasons why we give presentations: to have people remember the information we present. The chain of events in memory begins with attention. If your audience doesn't pay attention to what you say, the memory discussion is over.

Attention Precedes Comprehension

There has been a great deal of research on what an audience pays attention to and remembers from presentations and lectures. The results do not look good for most speakers. Attention is good for the first ten minutes of a lecture, then drops off sharply until the end. Research conducted at many universities shows that as attention dwindles, students decrease their note taking. The results of this research are quite disturbing for me as a University professor. Right after a lecture, students remember less than 40 percent of the information presented, and their retention drops to 20 percent after a week.

No attention, no retention.

What Was That? You must pay attention to the information coming in through your senses to plant it in long-term memory. Although this statement seems obvious, think about how many times you have read a boring or difficult book and noticed that although your eyes have scanned every word, you have no idea what you just read. Sometimes external events may have distracted you, or you may have been daydreaming, but the important point is no attention means no retention.

Putting Your Twelve Cents In. The following picture, taken from the website of the Exploratorium in San Francisco (http://www. exploratorium.edu/exhibits/common_cents/index.html) shows twelve pennies. See if you can pick the one that is the actual penny. Don't look at the answer until you have made your choice.

The correct one was A. So how does this relate to memory? You have been handling pennies all your life, yet you have probably never paid close attention to them. All you've ever had to do is know the difference between pennies and other coins. Although you could easily tell the coins in the photo are pennies (as opposed to dimes or quarters), in this case, it was probably difficult to pick the real one. This task would have been easier if we had conducted the demonstration as follows:

1. Provided instructions that explained the task, alerting you to pay close attention to actual penny features to distinguish them from fakes.
2. Given you a real penny to examine in preparation for the pictures.
3. Shown you the pictures.

Instead, you had to rely on your past attention to details about pennies. As a speaker, you can focus the audience on aspects of your talk with colorful details that stimulate attention and strengthen retention. This is much stronger than saying, "This is important," which diminishes the value of your statement and could create the opposite effect on the listener.

The Attention Factor. Many things affect an audience's attention. If you understand how they work, you can adapt your presentation accordingly. Here are a few key factors to pay attention to.

■ **Intensity:** Product marketing encourages the use of bright colors. Speakers raise their voice for important points. We notice what stands out. Reserve intensity for things that are essential. Many politicians are criticized because they shout about trivial as well as important points. When you make everything intense, you make nothing intense. We notice intensity because of *contrast.*

> When you make everything intense, you make nothing intense.

■ **Novelty:** Back when humans were all four-foot-tall hominids, Grog and Awg left their cave. Engaged in a heated dialogue about where to find their next meal, they failed to notice the saber-toothed tiger lurking nearby. The tiger pounced on Grog. You can be sure the next time Awg left the cave, he remembered Grog's last day, the time, the temperature, the smell of the tiger's breath, and the sound of claws scratching on rock. This attention to detail and memory of the event kept him alive. Thankfully, we don't have to worry about saber-toothed tigers today, but this same hardwiring drives audiences to remember more details from unusual stories, actions, and anecdotes than from predictable, factual material.

So the next time you are compelled to begin a presentation with "Thank you for having me" or "What I'm going to talk about today is" or "Isn't it great to be back in Las Vegas for our conference?" think again. There is nothing novel, surprising, or memorable about these openings. Because the audience has heard them before, they are not paying attention. Their survival is not at stake. But yours may be.

> Use colorful details to stimulate and strengthen retention.

■ **Incongruity:** Things that do not make sense within their context draw our attention. We attempt to solve the puzzle, which leads to our paying closer attention to these items. If you start your presentation with an arresting open, even though people don't immediately know its relevance to your topic, they listen carefully to what you say next. When you resolve the incongruity, they remember it.

My high school biology teacher announced to our hormonal class that she was about to place her hand on a boy's most important sex organ. The class was riveted. No one exhaled as she walked over to me. I blushed deep red with embarrassment. Then she placed her hand firmly on my forehead. The class got it, realizing that our brain is our most important sexual organ.

> Things that do not make sense in context draw listeners' attention.

■ **Personal significance:** The more important something is to us, the more likely we will pay attention to it. Magazines and newspapers use "pull quotes," which are quotations in very large type, usually set off by boxes or lines. They are intended to seduce people into reading a story by mentioning something they think will be of great interest. Look for new legislation, technological innovations, or recent events in the media that directly and personally affect your audience's interests.

▪ **Emotion:** Anything with strong emotional content is quickly noticed. When you read a story about a hostage kidnapped by terrorists, a child falling down a well, or miners trapped in a coal mine, you remember it. The media always devotes a great deal of space to news items like these. Make your anecdotes and stories more emotional.

> Make your anecdotes and stories emotional.

THE WAY IT WORKS

The latest cognitive findings reveal we can only focus on one complex thing at a time. What you focus on is not always the most important thing, but what is most interesting to you. A good example is what psychologists call the "cocktail party phenomenon." If you are talking to someone in the middle of a social event, there are generally several other conversations going on around you. If you had a decibel meter and measured their loudness, they would all be equal. But you have the ability to focus your attention and tune out the other conversations, so you can pay attention to the one you're in.

You may also hear snippets of a more lively conversation and find it difficult to concentrate because you are trying to listen to that one. Your goal is to have your presentation be "that one," the most engaging conversation in the room.

Gain Traction

Television directors and editors understand how to grab and hold an audience's attention, which is critical for their ratings. So that interviews don't become boring "talking heads," the rule of thumb is to limit interview responses to no more than twenty seconds. After that, it is essential to cut away to visuals or footage of what the interviewee is referring to. This change of angle and variety keeps the viewer engaged. Even so, the *total* time of one interview response *including* visuals is typically no more than forty-five seconds. Although media is more compressed and fast paced than live, it is a real indicator of what needs to be done to make sure viewers don't change the channel.

Ten-Minute Intervals. Prepare something dramatic, unusual, or interactive for every eight to ten minutes of your talk. This is about as long as humans can go without getting distracted. Include anecdotes, interactions, questions, and dynamic content to keep audience members' attention and make them anticipate what's coming next. This will also bolster your confidence because you can look forward to those moments and the audience's reaction to them.

> Break up your talk every eight to ten minutes to keep your audience engaged.

Grab Bag. Employ technology, breakout sessions, and interactivity to mix up your presentation. If there are visual aspects to your

Distractions

You can plan all you want, but often there will be distractions that are unexpected and out of your control. Computers will crash, car alarms will go off, someone will laugh in a high-pitched voice or have a coughing spasm. In the event that there is a loud noise, a strong odor, or a strange sight, repeat whatever you've just said. Do not assume that your point was heard during the distraction.

talk, don't just describe them verbally. Generate slides, pick up a prop, or draw on a white board. Make sure the visuals clarify or complement what you are saying.

Mental Recess. There is an old saying: "The mind can only retain what the seat can endure." Break your presentation into sections, with summaries at the end of each one. This will keep listeners mentally alert and engaged.

Counterintuitive Questions. Questions are one of the best ways to make a presentation interactive. Most presentations require little interactivity from listeners, so they remain passive. Be careful not to ask obvious questions that can appear patronizing to your audience, such as "How many of you want to have a better life?" By answering questions, individuals are engaged as they mentally attempt to solve the problem, apply it to their own experience, or come to the rescue of the speaker who is asking for interaction. Counterintuitive questions challenge, involve, and surprise the listener.

> Who do you think gets sued more often for malpractice—doctors who are incompetent but nice, or extremely competent doctors who act aloof? Since malpractice is based on competence, it would make sense that "nice" shouldn't enter into it, *but* research shows the direct opposite. People who judge their doctors as nice don't sue, regardless of their level of care. People who judge their doctors to be cold and distant sue more often, even if their doctors give them better care.

Questions like this involve the audience in three ways. First, when people make their prediction; next, when they hear that they are wrong; and finally, when they learn the rationale for the correct answer.

Hall Monitor. Observe listeners to see if they are paying attention or are fidgeting, looking at their watches, or talking to one another. When the connection between you and the audience is slipping, you must recapture it. Begin developing a repertoire of techniques to regain your audience's attention. At a minimum, always have a compelling story ready for these occasions.

> Always have a compelling story in your arsenal to recapture attention.

THE GATEKEEPER

Learning and attention involve both working memory and long-term memory. Once something is placed in long-term memory, researchers believe that it remains there forever. Working memory acts as the clearinghouse, or gatekeeper, to determine how and what gets stored in long-term memory and when it gets activated to solve a problem.

Working Memory

Since the 1960s, psychologists have used the phrase "short-term memory" to mean a holding tank for information we take in through our senses. Currently, psychologists believe that a lot more happens in short-term memory and refer to its expanded role as "working memory." This is where thinking takes place and corresponds to what we think of as consciousness. Working memory determines whether things get remembered or not.

It has two basic functions. First, it holds information for a short period of time. An example of this is when you are told someone's name as you are introduced. The name goes into working memory. You have about thirty seconds to transfer it to long-term memory or lose it forever. The second function is even more important. It's called thinking.

Making the Leap

There are two things to consider when transferring information into long-term memory: rehearsal and organization.

1. Rehearsal. This is a fancier way of saying repetition. Ironically, pure repetition leads to rapid forgetting. Information is lost easily unless you can create some form of organization or association for it. Rehearsal is usually inefficient because it is not organized in a way that allows you to recall things efficiently. Do you remember very much from your days of cramming the night before tests? The term "elaborative rehearsal" is used when repetition is combined with techniques that link the information to something you have already placed in memory. It works best when you can make new information personal. Elaborative rehearsal organizes information to make it useful.

2. Organization. The better you can organize information when you first place it in memory, the easier it is to retrieve later. Psychologist Richard Anderson made a good analogy. He said to think of long-term memory as a large, dark attic. If you have to find something in that attic, you must use only a small flashlight with a thin beam of light. That beam of light represents working memory.

> Pure repetition leads to lack of retention unless some form of organization or association is made.

Some people keep their lives, memories, and attics in great order. DVDs are arranged in alphabetical order; *National Geographic* magazines are bound by date; clothes are hung neatly by style, color, and season; and tools are neatly organized. Even with a little ray of light, any item can be found.

Other people have attics that are messy, and their memories are even messier. Their view is, "Just throw it up in the attic." They do this randomly without paying much attention to where things land. Later, when they prowl around trying to find something with their thin beams of light, it becomes extremely frustrating—and even worse under stress.

When you know a great deal about something, it is easy to organize it. For example, if your expertise is in financial planning and there is a change in the law, you know where to place this new information in your long-term memory. If you learn a new investment strategy, you know how to integrate it among your current skills and call it up when appropriate, which you cannot do when you are

Experience Matters

A vivid example of how organization works was demonstrated in a research study where the memories of chess masters were compared to those of intermediate players and beginners. If we showed a chessboard to a beginner and a chess master, who do you think had a better chance of remembering the locations of the pieces? The answer is—it depends.

In the experiment, each of the players was given two situations. One was a real chess game copied from a chess book, and the other had the same number of chess pieces randomly placed on the board. In the real game, the chess masters remembered the position of more pieces than the other two groups of players, but they did no better when the pieces were placed randomly. Their memories were no better in the random situation, but their knowledge of the game and the organization they identified enabled better retention in the real game.

first introduced to the idea of investing and all the possibilities are overwhelming.

This concept of organization is very important when making a presentation, because your audience is often composed of people who may be somewhat new to your subject. They hear your concepts but do not necessarily understand the organizational structure enough to store this new information efficiently. You must explain the framework in which it fits and how to remember it.

Do not assume that they will discover the organizational framework and relationships because you have structured your presentation well. Remember that a pattern is a pattern *only* if it is recognized.

Long-Term Memory

Some researchers believe that long-term memory retains information forever. It stores specific events like what you had for breakfast, general knowledge such as the names of state capitals, and procedures like how to multiply. Although information is stored for a long time, that doesn't mean you will always be able to access and retrieve it. Sometimes it's a person's name, a word, or where we put something, but we have all experienced not being able to remember, even though we had the answer on the "tip of our tongue."

Your audience will remember information best when it is thoroughly understood, organized, and integrated with knowledge they already have. This is because they have more organizational hooks to hang the new information on. However, information that you place in working memory lasts thirty seconds or less, so time is the enemy. You have to make each important fact or concept clear enough to transfer it to long-term memory before going on to the next topic or listeners will lose it. As a speaker, you can facilitate this transfer by linking the information to a story, a question directly related to their experience, or an example that would have changed the outcome of an event in their past. Processing in working memory allows you to reinterpret past events and make them clearer, change your causal attributions about these events, as well as store current information more efficiently because you understand how they fit into the greater scheme of things.

For example, you are assigned to give a talk to a group of non-technology professionals about the benefits and risks of e-commerce on the Internet. It is your job to use their prior knowledge about traditional commerce as the basis for showing them parallels to e-commerce. While your listeners may not understand concepts like firewalls and encryption, they *do* understand security codes and access procedures in banks. It is up to you to show them how e-commerce is analogous to each traditional business practice that they already understand.

> To implant information into an audience's long-term memory, link the information to a story, a question, or a specific example.

Identify areas in your presentation that contain a rapid sequence of new information that may be difficult for audience members to retain. Break up the information so they have time to process it. Either give them additional time to take notes, or add anecdotes or examples so they have an opportunity to transfer the information into long-term memory.

> Give your audience time and tools during your presentation to transfer information to long-term memory.

HOW MEMORY WORKS

Understanding how memory works will help you plan your presentation so that the audience will walk away with more information. For example, since working memory has such a rapid decay rate, if you jump from topic to topic, the audience will not have adequate time to transfer the information to long-term memory and will lose most of it. It's better to have fewer topics but spend more time on each so that ideas can be organized and processed more efficiently. You can begin with a quick story, then make the point that the story illustrated and then show how it's useful. This understanding of memory will make the point indelibly.

It's All About Me

Audiences remember less than you present, but they also remember more. Although this sounds like a paradox, there is a fairly simple explanation. They will remember less than what you say because they do not remember your words, only your ideas. In research studies, psychologists have demonstrated that people remember the substance of a presentation, not its form. (Remember the Carol Harris/ Helen Keller example presented earlier in this chapter?) Audiences also take away more than you said because as they listen, they combine what you are saying with what they already know. Your content will stimulate ideas that relate to things previously stored in each listener's memory. Because memory is constructive, no two members of your audience will take away the same information in the same way, even though they all heard the same presentation.

For example, if you are talking about the role accountants play in audits, audience members will hear and remember things differently depending on their background and experience with CPAs. Those audience members who have had stressful relationships with audits and accountants will interpret your words in one way, and those who have had good relationships and happy experiences, in another. In remembering the presentation, your words will be transformed to conform to the views each audience member had before he or she came to hear you. Think back to a time when you watched a presidential debate with a friend who backed the other party. When you discussed it afterward, it probably sounded like you listened to two different debates. Your assessment of the candidates was colored by what you believed about them before the debate began.

The Speaker's Role

There are times when audiences realize there is more information coming at them than they can process. As they realize they cannot get it all, they feel overwhelmed. Identify these potential trouble spots and provide additional information in a handout, or direct audiences to a website to visit later so they don't have to worry about missing key points.

Elaborative Rehearsal

As mentioned earlier, elaborative rehearsal connects new information to what has already been learned. This has the effect of personalizing the information and making it more meaningful. Elaboration gives your audiences more connections and more places to look when they want to find this knowledge later. It also decreases the likelihood that they will confuse it with other information stored in long-term memory, because it is now more distinctive.

Imagine you were delivering a presentation on how best to use the Internet for marketing and wanted to integrate elaborative rehearsal. You could break your audience into small groups and have them discuss how they could use the principles you've presented in their own marketing plans, identify the most successful examples of Internet marketing, or analyze unsuccessful ventures.

The more personal these activities, the better they will be remembered. The results of the discussions will be stored along with the information you presented. These breakout sessions should only last for a short time (two to four minutes). Giving audience members a short time actually fuels the intensity of their discussion and brings the focus back to you more quickly. Once you have regained their attention, ask for volunteers to report on new insights and how they will adapt those insights to their own marketing plans going forward.

Making Calculations

Instead of giving audiences information, have them make calculations or develop strategies to figure the information out for themselves. I worked with a client, Morris, who sold medical insurance plans to midsize companies. He would tell clients that a good medical plan would save money by reducing staff turnover. He devised a strategy that asked the audience to compute how much it cost to replace a manager, including headhunter fees, interview expenses, time spent interviewing, severance pay, and so on. Morris found that when listeners calculated the cost of losing an employee themselves, they decided it made a lot more economic sense to retain workers. They remembered the numbers they came up with better than they would have if the numbers had simply been presented to them.

Comparing and Contrasting

If you were presenting marketing strategies to improve branding, you would have audience members compare what they have been doing to the methods you've just introduced. Relating how this information is both similar and different from their prior knowledge is a good way to drive listeners to store new information in a well-organized way.

Paraphrasing

Asking audiences to restate concepts in their own words is a good way to make sure they understand what you are saying and place those concepts in long-term memory. You can either ask them to do it in writing during your presentations, or break them into pairs and have them take turns paraphrasing. There is an old saying: "The best way to learn something is to teach it." David pointed out that directors often ask actors having a difficult time with long monologues or soliloquies to paraphrase the speech, making sure they retain the sense of the wording.

Reaching a Conclusion

When you use inductive logic, give audiences several points and then ask them to come up with the conclusion that supports the data you have presented. This gives them a way to repeat the information while creating new connections to it. For example, list the costs of buying new computers every three years versus leasing them. After listeners sort out the data, they have to argue the merits of their conclusions.

Application

Applying principles is one of the best ways to ensure that audience members understand what you are saying at a deeper level. Writing it out also encourages them to think about it more deeply. Separating into small groups and presenting what they have written will increase elaboration.

Making Assumptions

Give audiences the task of generating assumptions for themselves. For example, I consulted with a company that created software to make Internet searches more efficient. One of their executives told an audience, "The average midsize company spends seventy-two thousand dollars a month on Internet searching." It was tossed out as a meaningless statistic because the audience couldn't relate to the figure. What I had him do instead was pose a few questions such as, "How many people at your company do Internet searches daily? How much time do these people average on their searches? What is the total average monthly salary for those people?"

He asked audience members to write these numbers down and do their own calculations. There were gasps in the room when they figured out the huge amounts of money they were spending. He achieved buy-in when they saw how much they could potentially save with a software product that saved employees time.

Automaticity (Also Known as Automatic Processing)

Your audiences perform two basic types of information processing as they listen to you: controlled and automatic. Controlled processing requires their full attention; it requires the engagement of all working memory, serious thought, and effort. Imagine that you and I were having a conversation as we were walking and then got into your newly rented car, one that was totally unfamiliar to you. What would happen to our conversation as you searched for the ignition, gearshift lever, and parking brake? Most likely, the conversation would come to a grinding halt as you tried to start the car, an activity that requires controlled processing and all of your attention.

Automatic processing requires very little attention, thought, or effort because you are so familiar with the task you are performing. It needs very little processing power from working memory. Using the same example, our conversation would not miss a beat if it were your car we were using. Driving your own car requires little effort because it is so routine and familiar.

When presenting, you need to repeat information in several contexts, relate it to various audience examples, and have listeners practice ways of remembering it to put them on the road to automaticity. You must know enough about your listeners to identify which areas they know well and which are new and require additional practice. If you place too much stress on audience members by constantly demanding controlled processing to follow your presentation, you will tire, distract, and lose them.

Position Placement

As we discussed in Chapter 3, the principle of primacy suggests that you are more likely to learn and remember the first thing that is presented. Nothing has happened before to interfere with the new information you are receiving. The principle of recency suggests that you also remember the last item presented because nothing follows to interfere with that information. Place the most important information at the beginning and end of your presentation for better retention. Things that are most easily learned and remembered should be placed in the middle.

Multimodal Repetition

Teaching is one of the best ways to learn and remember content. In a study of how actors memorize lines, psychologist Helga Noice and her actor husband, Tony Noice, asked participants to read scripts and focus on the meaning. When they had to explain the meaning to someone else, they remembered the words and concepts far more accurately than when they simply tried to memorize the lines. The Noices called this "active experiencing."

There is interesting research on what makes university students rate their professors high or low. I imagined it would be based on the grades the students thought they would receive for the course. I was wrong. Then I thought it might be how entertaining the professor was. Again, I was wrong. The major factor determining students' ratings of their professors was how much students got to talk during class. The more students participated, the higher they rated their instructors. Audiences like to participate rather than be passive.

Lose the Fat

In-depth coverage of a few concepts leads to far better understanding and longer-term retention than a superficial treatment of many topics. Most presenters look at how much time they have and then determine how much information they can cram into it. The best thing you can do is select no more than three to five key topics (three is optimal unless your presentation is longer than an hour), reinforce them in colorful ways, and suggest follow-up activities for audiences to obtain additional information.

> Focusing on no more than three to five key topics will ensure that your audience remembers your presentation.

IMPROVING YOUR OWN MEMORY

Sometimes you—and not your audience—have to remember things. Several factors determine how much information you can remember.

Time Elapsed

The more time that has passed since you learned or reviewed the information, the less you will remember. Your memory for any event is generally best right after it and decreases with time. If you are going to make a presentation and want to remember it well, make sure you rehearse as close to the day as possible. I always repeat my opening to myself as I'm walking up to begin a talk.

Information Overload

The more things you have to remember, the worse your performance will be. Organize the information well, break it into smaller sections, and work on learning each section. Spend extra time on the areas that are more difficult for you.

Performance Conditions

The closer the learning situation is to the conditions under which the information will have to be remembered or performed, the better you will do. Psychologists call this "encoding specificity." A dramatic example of this occurred during World War II. Soldiers learned to fire guns on target ranges at their base, but most of them couldn't make use of their training under the threat of enemy fire. Their retention was specific to one situation and could not be generalized. A large number of soldiers never fired their guns under battle conditions. Rehearse your presentation in an environment that is as

Don't Shoot the Dog

I was talking to a group of graduate students about instructional software design. The point I wanted to make was that when you are creating questions, you need to be careful not to make the feedback for a mistake more interesting than that for a correct response. I told them that during graduate school, I'd had a subscription to *National Lampoon*. When my subscription ran out, the publisher did not send me a typical form letter threatening to stop sending the magazine if I did not pay. Because they wanted to be cool, they sent me a postcard with the picture of a cute dog with a pistol pointed at its head. The caption read, "If you don't send us money, we'll shoot this dog!" I asked the students to decide whether that had made me send the money or not. It did not. It made me wait to see what they were going to do next. I was too curious to pay. They sent two more funny postcards before sending me a form letter asking for the money. I linked this anecdote to their experience by pointing out that when anyone tries to play a flight simulation program on the computer, the first thing they want to do is see what happens when they crash.

similar as possible to where you will be presenting, or visit the site early to practice in the actual meeting place. To reinforce encoding specificity with your audience, provide examples that are as similar to their experience as possible.

Mnemonics

Mnemonics are devices to remember rote information. A classic example is how children learning to read music remember the names of the lines and spaces of the treble staff:

Lines on the treble staff—"Every good boy does fine."
(notes E, G, B, D, and F)
Spaces on the treble staff: Face (notes F, A, C, and E)

Mnemonics are valuable because they introduce a form of organization to material that would ordinarily be learned as unrelated, rote information. Mnemonics make it easy for us to remember lists of information. This technique dates back to Greek and Roman orators.

Method of Loci

When Cicero went into the Roman Forum to give an oration, he had to have his long speeches committed to memory. He would associate a part of his speech with each column and archway, so that looking around the familiar enclosure would cue the next part of his oratory. Often, when you craft a presentation, you take a series of elements and string them together: talking points, stories, and transitions. It may be easy for you to remember each section in isolation because of your history with it but difficult to remember the order of the entire presentation.

The method of loci is particularly effective for memorizing the order of a speech. Write down each section of your presentation in order. Then associate each part with a section of the room (a locus) in which you will be speaking, if you know the room layout. If not, use another room you are familiar with and picture it in your mind. Use the arrangement order in the room to remember each section of your speech.

LOWERING ANXIETY

If public speaking makes you nervous, there are many ways to manage your anxiety level (see Chapter 6). Knowing you will remember what you are supposed to say is one of the best ways to reduce nervousness. Here are a few important tips to maximize your retention:

- Limit content to the most important factors.
- Structure key points so the way they flow together is clear (better organization).
- Prepare vivid stories and examples for each topic (elaborative rehearsal).
- Visualize how the audience will use your information (elaborative rehearsal).
- Practice giving the talk in conditions as close to those of the actual presentation as possible (encoding specificity).
- Relax because it's all under control (anxiety reduction).
- Envision receiving compliments on a presentation that shows your mastery of the information (fun).

11

The Final Word

R esearch from cognitive science reveals that people make decisions emotionally and then back up their decisions with rational thought. Based on these findings, it is imperative that speakers
include their perspective, passion, and values in any presentation. There is no better way to persuade your audience or achieve
buy-in.

Studies in emotional intelligence add another surprising element.
More than 50 percent of the impact of a presentation is nonverbal
including movement, gestures, and body language. Therefore we
recommend that speakers pay as much attention to the delivery of
their presentation, as to the preparation of content.

PREPARATION

As a psychologist, I know that people under stress go back to what
they know best. We call it the "default mode." Boxers know that
fights are won or lost in the gym when they are essentially improv-

ing their default mode. A boxer begins a fight, realizes he hasn't prepared for it properly, tries to change tactics under stress, and then takes a huge beating.

This chapter has three purposes: (1) if you are going to make a presentation, it will give you a checklist to guide your preparation; (2) it serves as a summary for the entire book; and (3) if you read this chapter today and you have to give a presentation tomorrow, it will act as a life preserver.

The Preparation Checklist

We have divided the preparation checklist into four sections:

1. The crafting of your presentation, when you prepare the basic elements
2. Rehearsal, when you pull it all together and practice
3. The ten-minute call, right before a presentation, when you focus on the task in front of you
4. Postpartum, when you assess how you did and consider what to do differently next time

CRAFTING YOUR PRESENTATION

In our experience, no one in business has enough time. To shorten your prep time, the following template can be followed to prepare for any presentation:

1. Determine your intention or what you most want to achieve.
2. Choose the role you believe will best serve you in achieving this intention.
3. Devise a compelling opening and learn it well. If the opening suggests a theme, incorporate it.

4. Select three to five talking points that support your intention, and think of anecdotes for each of those points. Consider how to transition from point to point.
5. If necessary, construct PowerPoint slides to support your content.
6. Craft your closing. Be sure it is in line with your intention and know it as well as your opening.

1. Identify and Clarify Your Intention

The word *objective* is sometimes used as a synonym for *intention.* Determine the outcome you want from your presentation. For example, your intention may be "They will see me as critical to the success of their business," or "We will partner together going forward." To achieve your intention, remember the following:

▪ **Make your intention action-oriented:** If your first response to "What is my intention?" is that you want to educate your client or audience, ask yourself, "If they are educated (or informed), then what will happen?" Keep going down another level until the final outcome is an action statement or persuasive outcome. Now you have your true intention.

▪ **Limit yourself to one intention:** Having too many intentions is like having no intention at all. One intention gives your presentation focus and a driving force; too many cause confusion for you and your audience.

▪ **Set your intention so that it is under your control:** If your goal is to generate business, make it very specific. For example, your intention could be to obtain a second meeting with a potential client, identify three qualified leads at a networking event, or speak on your topic area to establish the perception that you are a leader in your field.

2. Select the Role to Fulfill Your Intention

Your language and behavior need to be harmonious to make your role clearly identifiable to a client. Roles also provide defined parameters so that you don't speak as a visionary when you are presenting as a motivator. Roles have the added benefit of increasing your comfort level. Unlike an actor who is cast in a specific role, you can select one based on your experience or what you want to achieve. Assuming a role will require that you speak with authority, conviction, and assurance to be believable. However, like an actor who demonstrates congruent language and behavior, you must never "break character." Congruence adds to the audience or client's confidence in you.

3. Create a Compelling Opening

As a speaker, you have a thirty- to forty-five-second window, or honeymoon period, in which to capture the attention of your audience. The following guidelines will facilitate your passage through this critical phase.

- Reveal something about yourself or your perspective to give the audience a window into your thinking and values.
- For a brief opening, enlist a simile or metaphor to frame your content. Visual imagery, snapshots, or brief anecdotes serve as memory markers and create rich associations to stimulate listeners' imaginations.
- Quickly transition from your opening trigger to the subject matter of the presentation. The importance of your opening is revealed and amplified by its link or relationship to your topic.
- Avoid generic openings about why you are happy to be there, what you are going to talk about (you're already talking), or

thanking people in the audience, your sponsor, or client. If you must thank someone, do it after your compelling open.

- Do not begin with an apology that makes the audience uncomfortable. If you make a mistake, use self-effacing humor and move on.
- Do not tell a joke that asks the audience to laugh. Leave comedy to the professionals.

4. Choose Your Talking Points

We recommend no more than three to five talking points, depending on the length of your total presentation. These points can be expanded on or made clear with anecdotes or case studies and backed up with robust evidence. Ask yourself these questions when you choose your points:

- "Do they advance my intention?"
- "Are they consistent with my role?"
- "Are they emotionally persuasive?"
- "Is this what my audience wants or needs to know?"
- "Can they be described with effective imagery or examples?"

People pay attention and remember content longer when it is presented as an anecdote. If your objective is to generate more business from your presentation, your anecdotes should reflect how you successfully solved a problem for a client. A well-told anecdote conveys your point of view, demonstrates your competence, and highlights the relevance of your experience. A well-told story appeals to every personality type. And a well-told story is memorable and portable. Listeners will tell your story to others, a very efficient way to market your goods and services. Through such stories, you also convey valuable technical information that satisfies the audience's need to be informed while positioning you as the delivery vehicle, or authority.

5. Prepare a PowerPoint Presentation

PowerPoint is the most popular multimedia program used by presenters. If you want to or must use it, here are a few rules to keep in mind when preparing your slide deck:

- PowerPoint is best used as a storyboard. Place individual slides in your slide sorter and arrange them in an order that conveys a narrative with strong pacing and momentum. If a slide doesn't advance the story, cut it out.
- You are the interpreter or messenger of the PowerPoint information. In that capacity, consider the one idea you want the audience to take away from each slide.
- Include mostly graphics and a minimal amount of text. Make sure the graphics are high quality. Determine where pictures will be worth more than words and use them accordingly.
- Avoid using wizards to plan your PowerPoint presentation.
- Insert a blank black screen whenever you want to deliver an example or anecdote. You can use the *B* key to black out the screen or *W* to make it white.
- Avoid too much text on any one slide. If you have a number of points to make, consider building them one at a time or breaking them into multiple slides.
- Construct slides that place items above, next to, or around each other and show graphically how they relate to each other.
- Create brief titles that tease the content rather than spelling out everything on the slide.
- Keep your slides simple and visually appealing. You are the center of attention. Powerpoint is your backup and complement.

6. Craft Your Closing

Typically, speakers spend time and effort on their opening and the body of their presentation but fail to adequately prepare their closing remarks. What a lost opportunity. The end of a presentation demonstrates resolution. It is when you can best persuade audiences or clients to take action; to remind them of what has been discussed (typically called a recap); or to come full circle, revisit your open, and add one new insight in a bookend. This technique conveys that you knew where you were going all along.

Speakers also typically rush as they near the finish. Speed indicates that you can't wait to leave the space and also says, "Don't listen to me. What I have to say isn't important." Instead, slow down and make eye contact around the room. Reinvest your commitment. Let everyone know that you believe your content so they will too.

REHEARSAL: PRACTICING YOUR PRESENTATION

Now that you have crafted your presentation, we highly recommend that you practice delivering it. Actors always rehearse at length to be able to perform without sounding or appearing rehearsed. Here are a few areas to focus on.

1. Prepare Your Instrument

Your voice is the medium that carries your message to the audience. It requires nurturing and development. To guarantee that your voice will work effectively takes care and attention:

- To be clearly understood and able to project with or without a microphone, you need to unhinge your jaw, relax your throat, practice forming vowels and consonants, and bring oxygen into your facial muscles.

- Focus on your breathing to make sure you always have plenty of breath support. Try to begin each new point after a breath.
- Drink lots of room-temperature water and eat grapes or apples to lubricate your voice. Avoid any drying agents, including caffeine and alcohol. Also, avoid dairy products and bananas, which give your voice a "sticky" quality.

2. Expect the Unexpected

To eliminate surprises, check out your space before any major presentation or keynote. Whenever possible, arrive early and walk the stage, do a microphone check, and be aware of the position of the lights, seating, and screens for PowerPoint. If you cannot arrive early, contact a person on site and ask for details.

When rehearsing, practice in as close an environment as possible to the real setting. For example, if you will be using a podium, rehearse behind a bar or stool that is approximately the same height. If you are in a large space, rehearse outside or project your voice to replicate the same audio properties. Practice your content by delivering it out loud, rather than reading it to yourself.

Practice under distracting conditions. Even the most seasoned professional can be thrown off when a PowerPoint slide, remote, laptop, teleprompter, or projector fails. Or the decision maker has his arms crossed, looks stern, or abruptly leaves the room. Or the speaker has rehearsed moving around the stage but discovers that her microphone is anchored to the podium.

3. Use Movement

Consider movement as physical grammar, creating punctuation to your verbal statements:

- Use only physical movements that feel natural for you.
- Introduce and revisit your theme when standing in the center of your space.

- Move downstage, toward the audience, on an angle when you want to make an important point.
- Create intimacy by walking in a straight line toward your audience and lowering your voice.
- To deliver a list of items or demonstrate thinking out loud, walk back and forth on a parallel plane to the audience.
- Highlight a transition by moving to another area of the space.
- The larger the venue, the more physically emphatic and expansive you need to be.

Remember these tips when you are presenting with PowerPoint:

- Stand near or in a direct line with the screen. This makes it easy to gesture, and you won't have to turn away from the audience.
- When a new slide appears, wait a second or two before talking. This will allow the audience time to absorb the content, so you do not compete with it. Then to regain focus, make a move or gesture or raise your voice.
- Maintain your physical energy and enthusiasm. Don't let the big screen overpower you. You are still the lead performer, and PowerPoint is your backup.

4. Keep It Fresh

After you have given a presentation a few times or if you overrehearse, the words can become stale and sound lifeless or canned. With each practice, your brain is processing the order of your words and phrases. After multiple rehearsals, it begins to lock the specific sequence into memory. The litmus test is if you forget one word and are thrown completely, meaning you don't remember what comes next—then you know it's time to freshen it up. The same is true if you deliver a statement and hear the exact same phrasing, emphasis, and intonations you had the last time. Use new words and phrasing each time you rehearse to come up with unique expressions or unexpected concepts. And to keep your presentation fresh, mix up the items or phrases to breathe new life into them.

For example, the first paragraph that follows is a logical explanation of Eloqui services constructed in a more traditional format. The second version has been made more dynamic simply by reediting the order of the phrases.

Version 1

Eloqui is a business communication and training company based in Calabasas, California. I'm David Booth, a former actor and theater director, and cofounder of Eloqui. The Eloqui method is a combination of performance skills from the entertainment industry, blended with neuroscience research and impression management from psychology. At some point in nearly every corporate pitch, beauty contest, or prospective client meeting, it comes down to "Why you?" Eloqui's persuasive techniques ensure that our clients increase their hit rate and win.

Version 2

At some point in nearly every corporate pitch, beauty contest, or prospective client meeting, it comes down to "Why you?" Eloqui's persuasive techniques ensure that our clients increase their hit rate and win. The Eloqui method is a combination of performance skills from the entertainment industry, blended with neuroscience research and impression management from psychology. Eloqui is a business communication training company based in Calabasas, California. I'm David Booth, a former actor and theater director, and cofounder of Eloqui.

THE TEN-MINUTE CALL

Public speaking causes anxiety at varying levels for most presenters. The greatest anxiety appears a few minutes prior to a talk and during the first couple of minutes. There are a variety of relaxation techniques and exercises to manage anxiety and focus the mind prior to and during this critical period. They do not have to be executed in any particular order. Develop your own shorthand.

Bridging

Whether it has been a busy day at the office, you have been socializing with colleagues at your table, or you have been stuck in traffic and arrive only minutes before your presentation, give yourself time to bridge. *Bridging* means clearing your head and eliminating all distractions approximately ten minutes prior to your talk. Turn off your cell phone, Blackberry, and laptop. Write down anything you want to remember later or pass these tasks off to an assistant.

Do a sense memory exercise. Recall the sensory elements of an event that made you feel warm, confident, or bulletproof so that you exude the same qualities from the moment you encounter your audience.

Begin breathing slowly and deeply into your abdomen and repeat your intention to yourself. Do not try to replay your entire presentation in your head, but definitely rehearse your opening so you know it cold. Trust that you have the necessary experience and will be able to recall the remainder of your talk when you need it. This is an essential process to ensure a successful presentation.

POSTPARTUM

You may feel a letdown after your presentation. Most likely you have been preparing for this event for a long time. Then it feels like it's over in a heartbeat. Give yourself time to come down after a major presentation or pitch. If you are tired, cut yourself some slack. Putting your full attention on your audience and being focused on achieving your intention can be exhausting.

But you're not done yet. The time immediately following your talk is useful for improving your speaking ability and advancing your career. Ask friends or colleagues who were in attendance for their comments. Be specific in terms of what you want to know. For example, "What do you remember of my examples?" "Did I speak too quickly?" "What do you think my intention was?" "What impression did I deliver?" (e.g., capable, creative, or authoritative). Or, "How can I improve?" Critical comments from someone you respect are extremely valuable. It means the person cared enough to share his or her observations. Perhaps you rocked back and forth or licked your lips repeatedly and didn't realize it. You might have said there were three points you wanted to make but only covered two of them. You may have repeated "ums" or phrases such as "I'm going to talk about" too many times. Or your energy may have lagged in the last third of your talk and you lost commitment and focus.

Also, pay close attention to the questions you receive from the audience or client. They will give you valuable insights and reveal how you were perceived. For example, if you are asked for business advice, you have successfully projected your role as a trusted advisor. If you are asked to predict the future, you have been seen as a visionary or seasoned veteran. And if you are asked how a process works, most likely you have exhibited qualities of a facilitator.

To be an effective communicator, you need to establish a solid foundation. But this is only the first step. How long did it take you to become proficient at your current profession? Why should becoming a masterful speaker be any easier or less time-consuming? Mastery requires studying, implementing, and translating skills into your own lexicon—one step at a time. No one can absorb everything at once.

Becoming a great communicator is a fluid process. Once you become aware of your strengths as well as your weak points, you can correct or change behavior to be better next time. The goal is not to be perfect. The goal is to be authentic and engaging and to enjoy speaking.

Once you enjoy speaking, the world is your oyster. Like a sport you love, you will actively acquire new skills to improve your game. As your palette of tools expands, you will feel the thrill that actors experience on opening night or in the flow of a dynamic performance. And although growth of your business may be your applause, you will also have the inner satisfaction of moving others with a human being's most fundamental tools: your body, brain, and voice.

Appendix

Action Verbs

Use action verbs abundantly in elevator speeches, presentations and cover letters to promote achievements. They create strong impressions by suggesting visual images. Always include action verbs in solution statements.

Management	developed	led	scheduled
achieved	directed	motivated	strengthened
administered	encouraged	organized	supervised
analyzed	evaluated	outlined	united
assigned	executed	oversaw	
attained	implemented	prioritized	**Communication**
conceived	improved	produced	addressed
consolidated	incorporated	recommended	arbitrated
coordinated	increased	reevaluated	arranged
decided	inspired	reported	authored
delegated	launched	reviewed	communicated

corresponded
counseled
developed
defined
directed
drafted
edited
enlisted
formulated
influenced
interpreted
lectured
mediated
moderated
motivated
negotiated
persuaded
promoted
publicized
reconciled
reunited
renegotiated
reported
researched
summarized
spoke
translated
wrote

Research
clarified
collected
conceived
critiqued

detected
diagnosed
disproved
evaluated
examined
extracted
identified
inspected
interpreted
interviewed
investigated
organized
researched
reported
reviewed
searched
studied
summarized
surveyed
systematized
wrote
Technical
analyzed
assembled
built
calculated
computed
designed
devised
engineered
fabricated
inspected
maintained
operated

overhauled
programmed
remodeled
repaired
solved
trained
upgraded

Teaching
adapted
advised
clarified
coached
communicated
coordinated
defined
developed
enabled
encouraged
evaluated
explained
facilitated
guided
informed
initiated
instructed
lectured
persuaded
presented
set goals
stimulated
taught
trained
updated

Financial
adjusted
administered
allocated
analyzed
appraised
audited
balanced
budgeted
calculated
compared
computed
developed
estimated
forecasted
managed
marketed
planned
projected
reevaluated
reconciled
researched
sold

Creative
acted
applied
composed
conceived
conceptualized
created
designed
developed
directed

established
evaluated
fashioned
formed
formulated
founded
illustrated
instituted
integrated
introduced
invented
molded
originatcd
perceived
performed
planned
presented
produced
refined
rewrote
updated

Helping
advised
aided
assessed
assisted
brought
clarified
coached
coordinated
counseled
dealt
demonstrated

diagnosed
educated
encouraged
enlisted
expedited
facilitated
familiarized
guided
helped
inspired
maintained
modified
performed
referred
rehabilitated
represented
supported
upheld

Clerical
activated
altered
assembled
approved
arranged
catalogued
classified
collected
compiled
described
dispatched
edited
estimated
executed

gathered
generated
implemented
inspected
listed
maintained
monitored
observed
operated
organized
overhauled
prepared
processed
proofread
published
recorded
reduced
retrieved
screened
specified
streamlined
systematized

**Additional
Action Verbs**
anticipated
arbitrated
charted
checked
classified
collected
completed
conducted
conserved

consolidated
constructed
controlled
coordinated
counseled
created
defined
delivered
detailed
detccted
determined
devised
diagnosed
directed
discovered
dispensed
displayed
disproved
dissected
distributed
diverted
dramatized
drove
eliminated
empathized
enforced
established
estimated
evaluated
examined
expanded
experimented
explained
expressed

extracted	interviewed	recorded	supervised
filed	invented	recruited	supplied
financed	inventoried	reduced	symbolized
fixed	investigated	referred	synergized
followed	judged	rehabilitated	synthesized
formulated	led	related	systematized
founded	learned	rendered	talked
gathered	painted	repaired	taught
gave	perceived	reported	tended
generated	performed	represented	tested
guided	persuaded	researched	trained
handled	photographed	resolved	transcribed
hypothesized	piloted	responded	translated
identified	predicted	restored	traveled
illustrated	prepared	retrieved	treated
imagined	prescribed	reviewed	troubleshot
implemented	presented	risked	tutored
improved	printed	scheduled	typed
improvised	processed	selected	unified
increased	produced	sensed	united
influenced	programmed	separated	upgraded
informed	projected	served	used
initiated	promoted	sewed	utilized
innovated	protected	shaped	verbalized
inspected	provided	shared	warned
installed	publicized	showed	washed
instituted	purchased	sketched	weighed
instructed	received	solved	
integrated	recommended	sorted	
interpreted	reconciled	summarized	

Glossary of Terms

This glossary provides definitions of theatrical, cognitive science, and psychological words and phrases used in this book and by Eloqui in communication training.

aesthetic distance: The distance from the speaker to the audience. Determining this is subjective and dependent upon the size of the room. A speaker should never crowd listeners or make them uncomfortable, but if positioned too far from the audience the connection is lost.

amygdala: The oldest part of the brain. Novelty and surprise activate it, making it pay attention and record details. Also called the "fear filter" or "self-defense mechanism."

anecdote: A short account, story, or narrative of an event. Not to be confused with *antidote* which is used as a remedy to counteract the effects of a poison, like snakebite.

automatic processing: Thinking that requires minimal attention or effort because the task being performed is so familiar that it needs very little power from working memory.

automaticity: A state that is achieved when a task is so well learned that it requires almost no mental effort to perform. Actions like reading or walking are learned to a level of automaticity.

attention precedes comprehension: The concept of grabbing the attention of audience members or clients to ensure they understand and absorb the ideas you are presenting.

bookending: A device used in closing whereby the speaker uses a variation on the opening or refers back to it to complete the presentation.

breaking the fourth wall: Eliminating the invisible barrier between speaker and audience. Crossing downstage toward the audience, asking a question, or bringing a volunteer onstage are effective methods of breaking the fourth wall.

bridging: A preparation technique used just before speaking to move from the presenter's everyday self to assuming the role he or she has selected, while keeping the presentation's objective in focus.

bubble: The immediate space around a person's body that is under his or her control.

buttonhook: A cross from downstage to upstage in a semicircular fashion while maintaining contact with the audience.

chunking or bunching: A technique employed by speakers to frame information by grouping items or ideas into discrete sections for easy recall. Working memory can hold only about seven independent pieces of information at a time, so the area code 310 is chunked or bunched into "three-ten" which allows the remaining digits of a phone number to be more easily remembered.

cerebral cortex: The area of the brain, activated by visual details, that plays a key role in memory, attention, awareness, and thought. Approximately 30 percent is devoted to visual processing.

cocktail party phenomenon: The ability to filter out other conversations so a person can follow the one he or she is participating in or wishes to hear.

command presence: A person's air of authority and physical carriage that leads others to take commands from him or her; vital for leadership.

communication framework: What every idea needs to make it stick. The five steps outlined in the book *Made to Stick*, by Chip and Dan Heath, are: pay attention, understand/remember, agree/believe, care, and act.

constructed memory: A subjective process by which people place information in long-term memory in a way that is consistent with their view of the world.

controlled processing: Thinking that requires a person's full attention; working memory must be engaged for controlled processing to occur.

counter cross: When presenting in pairs, one person moves diagonally downstage toward the audience in front of his partner, the other moves behind her to assume a position directly across from her.

counterintuitive questions: Questions that misdirect the audience. Once the answers are revealed, listeners' interest is heightened.

cue pickup: When one partner in a group presentation finishes her thought, the partner recognizes the signal and begins to speak.

cue tightening: Shortening the time interval or length of the pause between presenters which produces a more energetic tempo. (Long pauses indicate thoughtfulness or a more serious tone.)

cuing: Signaling a partner or team member to speak by dropping one's inflection and putting a definite vocal period at the end of a sentence or phrase.

curse of knowledge: When a speaker leaves out key pieces of information because he or she knows an extensive amount about the subject and cannot imagine that the audience or listener does not.

diaphragmatic breathing: Taking air into the lower abdomen to create breath support for longer sentences or sections of text. Also called "belly breathing."

directing focus: Pointing to, looking at, or favoring a person or screen, so the audience's attention is directed to that object. Also called "controlling the eyeballs."

dissociation: Light-headedness or disruption of thoughts that results from speaker anxiety.

downstage: Toward the audience.

downward inflection: A vocal "period" indicating that a speaker has concluded a thought or statement.

drying up: Theatrical parlance for forgetting one's lines or script.

elaborative rehearsal: A technique in which new information is personalized to make it more meaningful and easier to connect to existing knowledge.

encoding specificity: In a learning situation, recreating the conditions under which the information/presentation will have to be remembered or performed in order to improve recall.

engineering perception: The ability of a speaker to manipulate the impression of how he or she is seen by the audience.

fear of acceptance: Stage fright based on the fear of not being liked or accepted by the audience.

fear of competence: Stage fright based on the fear of not being able to perform successfully in front of an audience.

fight-or-flight response: The reaction of humans when they perceive danger; the brain prepares the body to run away or to stay and fight.

In either case, the heart begins to pump more blood to the extremities. This is efficient for survival but dysfunctional in situations not involving mortal danger, such as speaking in front of an audience.

first chair: The person who is currently speaking in a group presentation.

flop sweat: A speaker's fear of not knowing whether he or she will be accepted by the audience.

flow: A state of total immersion in a task, completely free of distraction.

framing: The use of a visual image, simile, or metaphor at the beginning of a presentation to create reference points for the material that follows.

gap theory: Creating a gap in listeners' knowledge and then filling it. Also known as "breaking their guessing machine, then fixing it."

generalization (training): Hardwired assumption that people do everything in a similar manner, regardless of the venue.

glossophobia: (Term often used to refer to stage fright.) The fear of being found out as a fake or something one is not. Why being an authentic speaker is important.

handoff: Passing the baton in a group presentation; completing a thought and signaling a team member to pick up the cue.

impression management: A process to influence the perceptions people have by regulating and controlling the information they are given in social interactions or when speaking.

information overload: When the amount of information given exceeds what can be retained.

intention: A reductive, active statement—best not stated aloud—that sums up the primary desire of the speaker; for example, "I will convince you to take action on the merger." Synonymous with the term *objective*.

justified movement: Movement that has a purpose; the opposite of wandering aimlessly or moving simply to expel nervous energy.

lateral movement: Crossing back and forth on the stage, parallel to the audience. It should not be confused with pacing, which is unjustified movement.

lavalier: A small microphone clipped to a speaker's lapel, shirt, tie, or blouse.

long-term memory (LTM): Permanent information storage in the brain. Evidence seems to show that once information enters LTM, it is there forever, even though a person may lose access to it when trying to remember.

mask theory: Eloqui translates mask theory into choosing a role such as trusted advisor, motivator, or facilitator as a filter for delivering content, giving the speaker a cover to avoid feeling exposed and therefore anxious.

maximizing/minimizing: A logical thinking fallacy that ignores positive outcomes and makes negative outcomes overly significant.

mental simulation: The act of getting listeners to imagine themselves within the action of a speaker's story by use of specific, visual details. Also called "playing the movie in your head."

metaphor: The application of a word or phrase to an object or concept to suggest comparison, as in "life is but a walking shadow" or "the bud of youth."

method of loci: A technique for memory recall of a list of items in sequence by associating each one with a physical landmark in the presentation area or a familiar room.

mnemonics: Memory devices that aid in the retention of rote information. For example, "*my very educated mother just served us nine pizzas*" is a mnemonic for remembering the names of the planets in the solar system in order of their distance from the sun.

multitasking: Performing several tasks simultaneously. Evidence shows that this can only be done when one or more of the tasks are learned to a level of automaticity.

obstacle, solution, and benefit (OSB): An Eloqui storytelling template, designed for client anecdotes.

on the nose: Expressing emotion, delivering a line reading (actor's script) or content in a presentation directly, without subtlety.

overgeneralizing: A logical thinking fallacy in which a poor conclusion is anticipated based on a single bad event. Speakers experiencing anxiety often overgeneralize.

over the top (OTT) behavior: Exaggerated behavior that is greater than a situation demands; often exhibited by motivational speakers and bad actors.

physical grammar: The use of movement for emphasis; for example, to create an exclamation point by moving resolutely on an angle toward the audience.

playing the house: Theatrical term describing actors hamming it up or ignoring other performers for the purpose of receiving more attention. In business, speakers hog the spotlight by directing remarks exclusively to the potential client's decision maker and failing to include other members of their team.

priming: Activating left- or right-brain functions. Analyzing or listing data primes left-brain serial thinking for debate and argument. Stories, emotions, and shared values prime the right brain to facilitate decision making and buy-in.

principle of primacy: Items at the beginning of a list are easier to recall than later items, particularly when the information must be remembered in sequence.

principle of recency: Items at the end of a list are retained longer because there is nothing that follows to interfere.

pulling focus: Drawing the audience's or client's attention to oneself by virtue of physical gestures, movement, or eye contact.

putting a button on it: Making a definitive move to an area onstage, while delivering a statement, planting one's feet, and then staying put for a couple of beats to give an impression of certainty.

reframing: A cognitive therapy strategy for viewing an idea in a different, functional way. For example, viewing the physical symptoms of fear as excitement or demonstrating that the brain is firing on all cylinders.

repetitive gesture: A gesture that repeatedly draws the eye and is distracting.

role: A device for achieving intention; a filter through which a person speaks. The choice of role allows clear identification through congruence of behavior and speech.

salient details: Precise elements of an anecdote or a description that incorporate one or more of the five senses.

schema: Information stored in memory that can be accessed to understand new information, i.e., invoking concepts one already knows.

second chair: Any member of a team who is *not* speaking. Second chairs engineer audience assent by putting their attention on, actively listening to, and agreeing with the speaker (first chair).

self-monitoring: Internal examination of one's own performance or internal state, which interferes with speaking because it splits the presenter's attention.

semantic stretch: An overused word or phrase, such as *unique, problem solver*, or "thinking outside the box."

sense memory: Reconstructing an event through imagery of specific, tangible perceptions such as sight, smell, feel, sound, and touch for the specific purpose of exuding that emotion when needed. This emotion can be recalled at a later time to enhance a speaker's performance.

short-term memory (STM): The number of items a person can recall given a single exposure. For example, what you remember of a list of items to pick up at the market when told on the way out the door.

shrinking the room: Drawing the audience toward oneself by assuming a conversational, personal style to make the room seem smaller and more intimate.

simile: A figure of speech in which two distinct things are compared using *like* or *as*; for example, "like a knife through butter" or "as wholesome as apple pie."

stage directions: *Upstage* means away from the audience; *downstage* is toward the audience; and *left* and *right* are from the speaker's perspective.

state-dependent learning: Duplicating as closely as possible the actual space where or conditions under which a speaker will be speaking to make his or her rehearsal more effective.

statistics: Data that should be used sparingly to illustrate a relationship and give credibility to discussion points.

sternum placement: A point in the chest important for vocal resonance; used to create depth in the voice; also called "chest voice."

string bet: Finishing a sentence or thought to indicate that a team member should take over and then continuing, creating an uncomfortable overlap.

telegraph: A signal that something is about to happen. Anticipating an event, statement, or actions with physical "tells" such as gesturing with a head nod or indicating with your hand for your partner to take over.

upping the ante: When the speaker feels the audience's attention slipping, he makes his subject of vital importance, for the purpose of reengaging the audience.

upstage: Away from the audience, toward the rear of the stage. The slang term *upstaging* refers to grabbing attention by moving toward the back of the stage.

vis-à-vis: In stage terms, the position of two speakers standing on the same plane, neither upstage or downstage of one another.

visual literacy: Fluency in the construction and use of visual devices; a major consideration in deciding whether to use PowerPoint.

visual snapshot: A highly compressed image that expands in the listener's imagination because of the visual details embedded in it.

working memory: Both short-term memory and thinking occur here. Often when a problem must be solved, information is retrieved from long-term memory and used in working memory.

Index